The Ride Down Mt. Morgan

Arthur Miller was born in New York City in 1915. After graduating from the University of Michigan, he began work with the Federal Theatre Project. His first Broadway hit was *All My Sons*, closely followed by *Death of a Salesman*, *The Crucible* and *A View from the Bridge*. His other writing includes *Focus*, a novel; *The Misfits*, first published as a short story, then as a cinema novel; *In Russia*, *In the Country*, *Chinese Encounters* (all in collaboration with his wife, photographer Inge Morath) and *'Salesman' in Beijing*, non-fiction; and his autobiography, *Timebends*, published in 1987. Among his other plays are: *A Memory of Two Mondays*, *After the Fall*, *Incident At Vichy*, *The Price*, *The Creation of the World and Other Business*, *The American Clock*, *The Ride Down Mt. Morgan*, *The Last Yankee*, *Broken Glass* and *Resurrection Blues*. His novella, *Plain Girl*, was published in 1995 and his second collection of short stories, *Presence*, in 2007. He died in February 2005 aged eighty-nine.

Thiago Russo is a psychoanalyst, master and doctor in American Literature from USP (Universidade de São Paulo). His PhD thesis partly produced at the University of Louisville (Kentucky) about *Ride* was elected the best in the programme and was nominated best thesis at the *Capes Award* (one of the most prestigious of Brazil). He is one of the authors in the essay collection *Arthur Miller for the Twenty-First Century*, and is currently writing his post-doctoral thesis about Arthur Miller's one-act plays and their socio-political contents at USP.

Susan C. W. Abbotson is Professor of English at Rhode Island College, where she mostly teaches drama. She is the author of *Student Companion to Arthur Miller* (2000) and *A Critical Companion to Arthur Miller* (2007), and numerous articles on Arthur Miller and other modern and contemporary playwrights. Past President of the Arthur Miller Society, she now manages their website and Facebook page, and is the performance editor for the *Arthur Miller Journal*. She also authored *Thematic Guide to*

Modern Drama (2003), *Masterpieces of Twentieth Century American Drama* (2005) and *Modern American Drama: Playwriting in the 1950s* (2019). She has published articles on Sam Shepard, Tom Stoppard, Mae West, Tennessee Williams, Thornton Wilder, August Wilson, Eugene O'Neill, Lillian Hellman and Paula Vogel in a variety of books and journals.

The Ride Down Mt. Morgan

ARTHUR MILLER

With commentary and notes by

THIAGO RUSSO

Series Editor: Susan C. W. Abbotson

methuen | drama

LONDON • NEW YORK • OXFORD • NEW DELHI • SYDNEY

METHUEN DRAMA
Bloomsbury Publishing Plc
50 Bedford Square, London, WC1B 3DP, UK
1385 Broadway, New York, NY 10018, USA
29 Earlsfort Terrace, Dublin 2, Ireland

BLOOMSBURY, METHUEN DRAMA and the Methuen Drama logo are
trademarks of Bloomsbury Publishing Plc

This edition first published in Great Britain 2023

A catalogue record for this book is available from the British Library.

ISBN: PB: 978-1-3502-6135-8
       ePDF: 978-1-3502-6136-5
       eBook: 978-1-3502-6137-2

Series: Student Editions

Typeset by RefineCatch Limited, Bungay, Suffolk
Printed and bound in Great Britain

To find out more about our authors and books visit www.bloomsbury.com
and sign up for our newsletters.

Contents

Chronology vii

Introduction xi
Historical, social and cultural contexts xi
Genre and themes xiii
Play as performance xvi
Production history xviii
Academic debates xxii
Behind the scenes – Interview with David Esbjornson who directed
The Ride Down Mt. Morgan at the Public Theater in 1998 and
on Broadway in 2000 xxv
Further study xxvii

THE RIDE DOWN MT. MORGAN 1

Notes 83

Chronology

1915   Arthur Asher Miller born 17 October in New York City.

1928   Bar-Mitzvah at the Avenue M temple.

1934–38   Miller enters University of Michigan to study journalism, switches to English after receiving the University's Hopwood Award in Drama for *No Villain.*

1939–46   Writes a number of radio plays that air on US radio shows.

1940   Marries Mary Slattery.

1944   *The Man Who Had All The Luck* premieres on Broadway but closes within the week, though receives Theater Guild National Award. Not produced in UK until 1960.

1945   Publishes the novel *Focus.*

1947   *All My Sons* premieres.

1949   *Death of a Salesman* premiers and wins Pulitzer Prize. *New York Times* publishes the essay 'Tragedy and the Common Man'.

1953   *The Crucible* premieres.

1955   The one-act *A View from the Bridge* premieres in a joint bill with *A Memory of Two Mondays.*

1956   Divorces Mary Slattery. Subpoenaed to appear before HUAC. Marries Marilyn Monroe. Revises *A View from the Bridge* into two acts to premiere in UK.

1961   Divorced by Marilyn Monroe.

1962   Marries Inge Morath.

1964   *After the Fall* and *Incident at Vichy* premiere at the new Lincoln Center, US.

1965   Elected president of International P.E.N., an international literary organization.

1968   *The Price* premieres.

1987   Publishes *Timebends: A Life* (autobiography), which appeared as a Book-of the-Month Club popular selection.

1989   George H. W. Bush takes office as 41st President of the United States of America.

1990   Miller turns 75 and London revivals of *The Price* and *The Crucible*, directed by David Thacker; release of *Everybody Wins*, a film based on *Some Kind of Love Story*; television production of Miller's version of *An Enemy of the People* (1951) is aired on PBS's *American Playhouse.*

1991   Premiere of *The Ride Down Mt. Morgan* in London, directed by Michael Blakemore. A one-scene version of *The Last Yankee* produced off-Broadway.

1992   Publishes the novella *Homely Girl, A Life*. Op-ed piece for *The New York Times* titled: 'Get It Right. Privatize Executions' that will inspire the plot of *Resurrection Blues* (2002).

1993   Premiere of two-scene version of *The Last Yankee*. Bill Clinton takes office as 42nd President of the United States of America. Miller awarded the National Medal of the Arts, and a television production of *The American Clock* airs on TNT.

1994   The seminal essay, 'About Theater Language', accompanies the 1994 publication of *The Last Yankee.* Premiere of *Broken Glass* in the US and UK; in the UK it won the Olivier Award for Best Play.

1996   Revised version of *The Ride Down Mt. Morgan* is presented at the Williamstown Theatre Festival (Massachusetts) with J. Murray Abrams as Lyman.

1998   *The Ride Down Mt. Morgan* opens at the Public Theater, directed by David Esbjornson with Patrick Stewart as Lyman.

1999   *Death of a Salesman* is revived on Broadway with Brian Dennehy for the play's 50th anniversary, and wins Tony for Best Revival of a Play.

2000   Broadway revival of *The Ride Down Mt. Morgan*, again with Patrick Stewart.

2002   Death of Inge Morath.

2005   Miller dies of heart failure in his Connecticut home on 10 February.

Introduction

Historical, social and cultural contexts

Arthur Miller has been remarkable both *on* and *off* stage. His life, stamped by activism since his college days, is testimony of a voice that remains one of the most powerful on an international level. From America to Europe, from Africa to Asia, Miller's transnational and transhistorical voice has been a source of reflection, discussion and, above all, change. Miller's anti-nihilistic position has always put him in the spotlight of hope in spite of a world that more and more casts its shadows over people and their lives. Miller's plays, short stories, novels and poems encompass some of the most pressing issues of the day and their power resides in the dramatist's capacity to explore both private and public implications. His political theatre not only shows what society is, but also what it could – or should be – had people been more attentive concerning their actions and what (to some extent) has propelled them to do what they do.

Miller's theatrical power has to do with a strong understanding of people in relation to the system they inhabit, a vision that helps explain why to some he was regarded as Un-American. His unmasking of one of the most powerful narratives of the United States, the American Dream, is at the core of Miller's private and public life. What is really amazing in his plays is that he does not break away from the past – as one might expect, looking at the theatrical avant-garde movements of the 1960s for instance that scorned it – but uses it as a rather powerful weapon to understand the present and change the future.

It is in resorting to the past that Miller wrote *The Ride Down Mt. Morgan* (1991/1998) looking back at the 1980s, a decade that still plays a fundamental role in current times where capitalism and the market continue to be mighty. First, Prime Minister Margaret Thatcher in the UK (from 1979 to 1990) and right after her, Ronald Reagan, 40th President of the United States (from 1981 to 1989) who promised to 'Make America Great Again', set in motion neoliberal policies that changed the cultural, social, political and economic landscape of their locations, giving rise to a strong neoconservative wave that has swept the globe ever since. While the 'Iron Lady' (Thatcher) declared that 'there was no such thing as society' and placed strong emphasis on individual efforts, Reagan defended a *laissez-faire* version of capitalism in which the defence of the business class, deregulation of the financial sector, and cuts in social programmes were a strong mark of what became known as 'Reaganomics'.

The Reagan Era was mainly characterized by the conservative ideology which celebrated rugged individualism and materialism as virtues, and profit-seeking became the holy grail. This fundamentalist view empowered corporations, made the rich richer, and disenfranchized many other people, a scenario inaugurated in the 1980s which has stretched until today. Consumerism and materialism were publicly hailed as signs of prosperity and were also backed up by Reagan's idyllic (and untrue) speeches of optimism about the inevitable progress of people which absolved individuals of responsibility to and for society. Sheldon Wolin states that the Reagan era embodied 'a political culture in which lying was merely one component in a larger pattern wherein untruthfulness, make-believe, and actuality were seamlessly interwoven'.

The cultural productions of the time mirrored the national narrative: the cinema witnessed the rise and success of movies like *Die Hard*, *Rambo*, *RoboCop*, *Terminator* and others, while reinforcing and celebrating stereotypical masculinity. Theatrical productions, and on a large scale the commercial theatre of Broadway, also reflected the national narrative in shows that exhibited glamour in productions with extravagant superstructure (involving special effects, music, dance and huge settings), while erasing from the stages and the public debate, issues such as poverty, race or abortion. The biggest hits of the decade were shows that still today sound familiar to many and that get revivals all around the world such as *Cats* and *The Phantom of the Opera*.

On the other hand, there were a few plays that dared to critique the 1980s essence of unfettered greed and materialism, such as Paula Vogel's *The Oldest Profession* (1981); David Rabe's *Hurlyburly* (1984); David Mamet's *Glengarry Glen Ross* (1984) and *Speed-the-Plow* (1988). A little further on, in the 1990s, Tony

Kushner's *Angels in America* (1991) and Arthur Miller's *The Ride Down Mt. Morgan* (1991/1998) offered caustic critique to the ideology of the earlier decade.

Reagan's position while in office blended a mixture of fantasy and reality with the aim of achieving what he saw as the American Dream. He frequently lied, especially claiming not to know that the US had sold weapons and missiles to Iran, and also supported guerrillas in Nicaragua in a scandal known as 'Iran-Contra'. He notoriously mixed stories he claimed to have lived but were actually scenes from movies he had acted in or watched.

When Miller wrote *Ride* he dialectically interwove its form (farcical tone, use of irony, flashbacks, dreams, memories and tragic elements) with the content (the critique of the eighties man and the decay of ethical and moral values promoted by neoliberalism), turning the play into a diagnostic of that era that had changed America (and the world) forever as well as offering a prognostic of what it might become afterwards.

At a time when the world has finally been contesting some of the most enduring untrue narratives of their countries through different social movements such as Occupy Wall Street, Black Lives Matter, LGBTQIA+, Feminist, and Environmental movements, and so many others, Miller's voice emerges as an encouraging one which interrogates several established national myths and unravels their very dynamic. The play you have in your hands is a powerful source of insight, reflection and transformation in a world that more and more has been showing signs of such a desired effective transformation.

Genre and themes

Ride is a very provocative play because of its form, but also its content. From its London premiere in 1991 to its 1998 New York production, the script evolved and several changes were made. The edition we are looking at is the revised and definitive version. Miller struggled with the form of the play because of its interwoven style that blends comedy and tragedy, turning *Ride* into a farcical tragedy. The play shows a man's deeds fuelled by blurred perceptions of reality – his commitment to himself and to his pleasure in a culture where lying was justifiable as long as it secured a sense of achievement. The central concern of the play is to show the dynamics of lying and its consequences, understanding it not merely as an individual act, but as one with devastating consequences for people and the collective sphere.

Inserted in a culture marked by materialism, greed, toxic masculinity and an emphasis on lying and deceit, *Ride* becomes an interesting diagnostic of the 1980s American Dream, as well as a picture of the socio-political forces that conditioned it. The play unfolds with Lyman's actions and speeches swaying between real time and evoked or staged memories/fantasies/dreams – a similar situation to that of *Death of a Salesman* and *After the Fall* – that attempt to justify or excuse his own life. The tragic dimension of the play lies in the fact that the tragedy that befalls the two families of Lyman is also the tragedy of a society that deceives, lies, manipulates and even takes pride in such acts.

The play opens in an extremely Reaganesque way: Lyman's first line being part of his dream/memory commands the ladies to cross their legs and then asks them not to do it, showing right away his traditionally arrogant masculinity and sexual drive towards women. Subsequently he says: 'I want you to look at the whole economic system as one enormous tit. [. . .] So the job of the individual is to get a good place in line for a suck [. . .] which gives us the word "success"'. This metaphor is at the core of the conservative ideology boosted in the 1980s and scorns (through the use of humour and a pun) citizens who need help from the State by criticizing people who 'suck' things out of it while they should provide for themselves. More of this ideology is unravelled when Lyman discovers his nurse is black: 'I've got the biggest training program of any company for you guys. And the first one that ever put them in sales'. Lyman celebrates the fact that as a businessman (one of the most cherished classes in the Reagan era) he has promoted inclusion, which is also a reminder that there is no need for the State to do it. The myth of the self-made man is celebrated through Lyman's pride in 'saving people' when he brags 'Here I start from nothing, create forty-two hundred jobs for people and raise over sixty ghetto blacks to office positions when that was not easy to do'. Nevertheless, when the play advances he admits he had done that in his youth because he was then a righteous man, but now finds himself a middle-aged, unrighteous man who has directed his energies inwards. This statement also mirrors the country's attitude backed up by neoliberal policies that encouraged self-realization by all means necessary.

Miller's use of irony, so typical of satires, throughout the play, works as a powerful comment on aspects of the Reagan era as well as a resource that unmasks Lyman and his attempts to remain naive. When Leah (in Act 1, Scene 2) reveals the desire to end her pregnancy, Lyman tells her that the baby 'has a horoscope, stars and planets; he has a *future*!' Such appeal seems humorous but it gets serious when one learns that President Reagan himself consulted a Californian astrologer regarding key decisions of the White House, though he denied it had any kind of influence on his policies.

Irony causes a comical effect since what is said or understood is the opposite of what it should be, and it is enhanced by the farcical atmosphere of the play. Farces bring forth absurd improbable events (two wives meet at the hospital and find out about their common husband); miscommunications (while a wife refers to her fearful husband the other refers to her fearless – and same – one), and physical humour (Lyman tries to hide under the bed sheet, closes his eyes, bangs his knuckles against his head).

In *Ride*, even guilt is widely explored through farcical scenes and dialogues. In an iconic scene (Act 2, Scene 2) Lyman faces the lion in Africa and defeats him by 'vomiting' onto the animal several motivational clichés about his own desires and refusal to be constrained, not even when it comes to monogamy. Trying to present himself as invincible and virile (in the style of *Rambo* or *Terminator*) he rationalizes his wrongdoing so as to justify his victory over guilt. Later on, when he explains his motivation for taking Leah to see (even from a distance) his supposedly former wife, Theo, by saying: 'I was dancing the high wire on the edge of the world . . . finally risking everything to find myself! Strolling with you past my house, the autumn breeze, the lingerie in the Madison Avenue shop windows, the swish of . . . wasn't it a taffeta skirt you wore? . . . and my new baby coiled in your belly? – I'd beaten guilt forever!' The farcical absurdity here lies in the fact that he describes his mischief in a highly poetic tone even when he hoodwinks those he claims to love and even worse: by describing it all proudly and narcissistically (find myself, my house, my new baby). The farcical elements of *Ride* end up by being tragic because by riding down Mt. Morgan (also a possible homophonic allusion to *Mt. More Gain*) Lyman drags down everyone around him, forcing them to see his real face and more painfully, the face of society. *Ride* powerfully reflects the essence of critical deeds of the political culture of the US, from Reagan's deceitful lie in the Iran-Contra affair to Bill Clinton's sex scandal with Monica Lewinsky.

Play as performance

Ride is a memory play that switches back and forth from memories to dreams/fantasies to real time. It follows Lyman Felt's mind as he becomes the director of his own play: he commands the women to lie down, he gives them lines, and interprets facts subjectively while he projects his own defence. This outline shows that Miller has turned away from realism, a trait with which he is frequently associated, and that becomes a bit of a problem for him in the United States. While Americans were too attached to the notion that Miller was a realist writer (and had been praised for it), the British, by and large, have been the ones who see Miller's later plays as visionary works of a master, while American critics have been reluctant and wary towards them, frequently dismissing them and asking Miller to return to a 'lost Eden'. Drama specialist Gerald Weales once pleaded (on the occasion of the premiere of *The Archbishop's Ceiling* in 1977): 'I will settle for the playwright of earlier days. Come home, Arthur Miller, and rediscover the American Maya.' Part of the rejection of Miller's late plays in the US is also due to the nature of the dramatic experience: while theatricality and emotional potential count a lot for Americans, the dramatic tradition in England is more linguistic and mental (think Coward, Pinter, Shaw, Shakespeare or Stoppard). That helps explain why Miller's post-1956 plays have had a hard time becoming hits in the United States whereas they have found a ready audience elsewhere in the world, especially in England, France and Germany.

That being so, performing a play like *Ride* poses a double challenge. The form of the play, which blends comedy and tragedy while time and scenes also overlap and lines between fantasy and reality are often blurred, is difficult enough to stage, but also the content of the play is challenging, as it introduces us to complex moral dilemmas with many implications and connections to wider spheres. This style of projecting memories/dreams/fantasies onto the stage is one that Miller had tackled before in plays like *Death of a Salesman* (which initially would be titled *The Inside of His Head*) and *After the Fall* (which recreates on stage fluid memories of its protagonist, Quentin). It is worth mentioning that while *Salesman* is considered the play that put Miller at the heart of the American stage, possibly *After the Fall* was the one that drove him out of it. One of the reasons *After the Fall* was so controversial lies in the complex form of the play that intends to piece together fragments of the protagonist's life and marriages (one of them seen as a reference to Miller's second wife, Marilyn Monroe, who had passed away shortly before the play opened). Miller, however, explains that *After the Fall* 'was about how we – nations and individuals – destroy ourselves by denying that this is precisely what we are doing'.

This explanation is at the core of all of Miller's plays and it aims at a better understanding of the current situation by taking into account what has been done, what could have been done, and what should have been done. Reading *Ride* poses a challenge because readers have to picture the changes in speech and acting areas (pointed out in the script), but for those who perform or watch it, such features become visual and artistically engaging. Readers and audiences alike might have some challenges distinguishing between the real and the imaginary (since this is a recurrent feature of Miller's late plays) and it gives the audience an enticing task to sort things out, with a formal structure that is a constant reminder of T.S. Eliot's concept of 'The Presentness of the Past'. While Miller seems to show us the chaotic state of the post-modern contemporary world in which we live, he also shrewdly translates that idea into the heart of the play's form.

An example of this innovative dynamic in which the past floods the present is when things start to get out of control, such as when Lyman's actions are reprimanded by the women in the play, he immediately 'cuts' the scene and evades a deeper reflection, by creating his own version/interpretation of the facts in a very farcical way. However, the more Lyman tries to escape from judgement, the more revealing the situation gets. In a scene where Bessie, the daughter, is destroyed by the idea that her father is hospitalized, Theo, her mother, commands her to 'think of Africa' as a way to resort to a happy and safe moment. This same moment, however, will be invoked later and will reveal the anatomy of Lyman's invincibility and boldness expounding this not-so-happy memory. It is precisely these features of flashback and interruptions that help audiences connect the puzzle and see what lies beneath such an apparent heroic act of facing a lion.

Since *Ride* is a play that shows different points of view, it turns readers, performers and audiences away from numbness while constantly subverting, denying or stating many aspects of the plot. Thus, for those who think of Miller solely as a realist playwright, *Ride* bespeaks Miller's mastery of a form that is both challenging and enriching for whoever pins hopes in a theatre with powerful range.

Production history

When Miller decided to open *Ride* he took into consideration the possibilities for the play to be not only praised but also understood. The commercialism of Broadway and its hard time embracing plays that dealt with more serious issues and challenging aesthetics was always criticized by Miller. He voiced against the Great White Way's *modus operandi* in a series of interviews and op-ed pieces everywhere, and had several of his late plays open outside the United States. Reinforcing this trend, Bigsby comments that several contemporary male American playwrights, such as Neil Labute, Sam Shepard, Tracy Letts and Wallace Shawn, started their careers in England, finding outside their native land a more welcoming audience that seemed to understand and better enjoy their plays.

Ride premiered in London in 1991 to mixed reviews. In the United States it was not produced until five years later, in 1996, at the Williamstown Theatre Festival, with slight changes in some lines. Some two years later, *Ride* had a limited run in New York City in 1998, and a subsequent Broadway opening in 2000. A film version of the play starring Michael Douglas was considered – written and directed by Nicole Kassell – but it was unable to get off the ground.

Directed by Michael Blakemore, the first performance of *Ride* ran at the Wyndham Theatre in London from October 1991 to February 1992, with Tom Conti, Gemma Jones and Claire Higgins, respectively as Lyman, Theo and Leah Felt. Critics and reviewers bid welcome to Miller's then-new play but mostly shared the feeling that this was not his best endeavour. There were varied aspects they targeted: the plot was flawed and full of ambiguities, the comic gist of the play bothered and confused some, while others were discontented with the casting and the production. While the female leads had been praised for their roles, Tom Conti had a hard time finding the tone for Lyman and played the part in a rather charming way which provides only one aspect of such a complex figure. Michael Billington, Britain's longest-serving theatre critic who writes for The *Guardian*, acknowledged the play's quality but lamented it was not 'vintage Miller'. Richard Christiansen writing for *Chicago Tribune* acknowledged the formal structure of the play as dialectically related to its topic suggesting that 'Realizing that bigamy is often a springboard for farce, Miller has peppered the play with wisecracks and gags as Lyman tries to cope with his past', but also 'an artistically unresolved play in a profoundly unsettled production'. There were others, however, such as William Henry who, writing for *Time* magazine, considered *Ride* as 'theatrically bold and intellectually subtle' and John Peter, the chief drama critic for *The Sunday Times*, who praised the cast and quality of the play, asserting that 'Miller is writing with all the vigour and agility of the commercial theatre at its most irresistible. This is the funniest play he has written. But it is an acid laughter, too, a laughter of bitter wisdom, and under the comic trimmings a serious moral and psychological argument is going on'.

The American premiere of the play in Massachusetts at the Williamstown Theatre Festival in 1996 was directed by Scott Elliott and was relatively well received. Having F. Murray Abraham, Michael Learned and Patricia Clarkson as Lyman, Theo and Leah Felt, respectively, the play fared well. Critics had an overall positive look on the play and praised Learned as cool and acid, but they felt that the production made it look as though the wives were gullible to get involved with Lyman, whilst overemphasizing the comedic/farcical tone by having Leah and Theo dressed like Playboy bunnies (Act Two, Scene Two) duelling with chipmunk voices about their cooking duties.

Notwithstanding some snags in the production, the play had Ben Brantley from *The New York Times* praising Miller for his 'constancy of vision' and 'willingness to experiment' and suggesting that while its moral seriousness is comparable to that of *After the Fall*, this might be Miller's first genuine comedy. Ed Siegel, writing for the *Boston Globe* found the play 'an accomplished, forceful piece of playwriting' and Robert Brustein, writing for the *New Republic* qualified the production as 'engaging' and 'an exhilarating journey'.

The play would return to the theatrical scene in the United States two years later, in 1998 (for a limited run at the Public Theater) and in 2000 (on Broadway's Ambassador Theatre), this time with a revised script that would become the definitive version of the play. The revisions mostly made the transitions between scenes smoother and easier for audiences to follow. Structural changes were made with the elimination of the character of Lyman's father (a ghostly presence that reminded the protagonist he should pursue the American dream and not to be a failure), as well as references to Lyman having one more child with another woman. The end was also slightly adjusted to suggest the protagonist is closer to an understanding of his situation, and an explicit reference to Ronald Reagan was eliminated, perhaps to make the script less dated. In spite of this latter elimination, Miller makes the end more fitting to the Reaganesque optimism, with Lyman's last words being: 'Cheer up!' despite the fact everyone has just abandoned him.

Directed by David Esbjornson, the first New York production had Patrick Stewart, Blythe Danner and Katy Selverstone as Lyman, Theo and Leah Felt, and they kept the same cast, but with Frances Conroy replacing Danner for the Broadway season (due to family concerns Danner could not take on the part for that season). Unlike Abraham who played Lyman at Williamstown as a reptilian whiner, Stewart displayed a more elaborate character whose facial shadings of ambivalence undermined his character's apparently confident assertions. The staging on Broadway kept the same off-Broadway crew, and with a bigger budget expanded the production with an amplified setting, more expensive costumes to better characterize the characters as upper middle class, and transitions between scenes were more dynamic and choreographed. While Frances Conroy's portrait of Theo as a deeply wounded woman was extolled and named as proof that there can be more to Miller's women than meets the eye, some critics were not happy with Stewart in the lead role. The first production of the play in 1991 had presented issues with Tom Conti, who according to Bigsby 'seemed to have considerable difficulty in bridging the different aspects of Lyman Felt's admittedly quixotic character'. A similar complaint to Billington's earlier one on the premiere, that the play was not 'Vintage Miller', was now made by American critic Bruce Weber, who comparing *Ride* to other Miller's plays asserted that '"Mount Morgan" doesn't pack the gut punch of any of those, but it is a pretty good poke in the side'. Overall, however, as Bigsby tells us, reviews 'reflected the success of a production that managed to sustain a tension between the humorous and the tragic, the vulgar and profound'.

Stewart, who was intensively besotted with the play and the character, explained that one of the scenes that excited the audience most was that of the lion. In an interview on the *Charlie Rose* talk show he recounts that 'The lion has appetite and nothing else. Lyman has not been able to satisfy his appetite without feeling the guilt that goes with it. He has never been utterly free. The encounter with the lion frees him from his guilt'. Such explanation undoes a lot of the confusion that befell critics and audiences alike, for the scene had seemed to many absurd, unrealistic and far-fetched (Stewart even mentions that there were talks about having it removed from the play). However, this crucial scene is one in which the penny drops and we get to see deeper layers of the plot. Stewart also reveals that 'I remember sitting in a coffee shop on the Upper East Side and two women came over to me, very angry. I had to assure them that I was only acting the role. Lyman is a dangerous individual. He has a devastating effect on at least three lives'. Watching such a play does not provide easy answers or solutions, but it can stir whomever reads, watches or performs it, leaving no one unscathed.

In 1999, *Ride* was a nominee for a Drama Desk Award (Outstanding Play and Outstanding Actor, Stewart) and also for the Tony Award in 2000 (Best Play and Best Actress, Conroy). The play had successful German productions right after the London's premiere in Dresden and Frankfurt in 1992 and continues to draw attention of readers/audiences around the world due to its fascinating/ complex form and thought-provoking theme. Many countries like Argentina, Brazil, France, Iran, Mexico and others have successfully produced the play and testified to Miller's appeal around the globe.

Academic debates

Even though *Ride* is not part of the 'Big Four' (*All My Sons, Death of a Salesman, The Crucible* and *A View from the Bridge*), it has nonetheless received some academic attention as to its themes and style as well as its relevance. Scholars have reflected about this farcical tragedy through different approaches and have pointed out varied implications of Lyman's deceitful acts. While some investigate its philosophical/psychological/existentialist implications, others go a step further, taking all of these dimensions into consideration, but also the socio-political atmosphere that frames the play. Identifying the play's provocative perspectives that often lie under the surface, helps to enhance the comprehension of this powerful play as well as bring enlightenment to other plays of Miller.

Dwelling on the philosophical/psychological/existentialist implications of bigamy, Terry Otten, Robert Scanlan and Steve Centola offer interesting and innovative views. Otten asserts that Lyman Felt could be regarded as a pre-Fall Adam encircled by luring Eves and goes on to analyse the tragic/mythical dimensions of the play. Robert Scanlan points out that *Ride* embodies an intense debate about love, sexual desire and marriage, and underlines that betrayal stands on the opposite side of responsibility and fairness. He also praises the potential of this late play mentioning that it 'might arguably have far more social and psychosexual significance than does (or did) the melodramatic *A View from the Bridge*', so the play remains somewhat of a hidden gem. Fitting the play into a category he names the 'damaged wives' series along with two others, *The Last Yankee* (1991/1993) and *Broken Glass* (1994), he emphasizes how *Ride* is not only about bigamy itself, but about its devastating moral implications. From the existentialist standpoint, Centola offers an insightful perspective on the play resorting to Jean-Paul Sartre's concept of freedom. He underscores the various facets of the play's central issue of betrayal, and insists on Miller's artistic grandeur and thoroughness when approaching such a topic.

Dwelling on the political dimensions of bigamy Christopher Bigsby, Jeffrey Mason and Susan Abbotson offer further insights. Bigsby points out that the play was, in part, a response to Reagan's America. This is a moment in which not solely money, but an 'imperial self' became victorious (unsurprising since, as mentioned earlier, major productions of the decade were films like *Die Hard*, *Rambo*, *RoboCop*, and *Terminator*– all hailing a cult of masculinity and power as the goals of life). Bigsby also points out that Lyman was a man who believed he could have everything and not pay the price – even comparing him to F. Scott Fitzgerald's Jay Gatsby – in a decade in which that brazenness seemed to have become an article of faith. Thus, Bigsby sees the play and its central action (Lyman's cheating) not merely as an expression of a character that acts out of pure desire, but as a product of the system into which he is inserted. We are once again in the face of a Miller play in which characters abandon compromise, commit themselves to their feelings and desires, but eventually will have to come to terms with their decisions and actions. Miller used to say that his plays were about 'the chickens coming home to roost' and this has been his trademark since *The Golden Years* (1939–1941) up to his very last play, *Finishing the Picture* (2004).

Another interesting perspective comes from Mason, who insists on the idea that in Miller's plays, and especially in *Ride*, one should see 'The personal as political'. He explores the dynamics of Lyman's relation to the women by constructing an anatomy of how the protagonist exploited both Theo and Leah for his own benefit, reproducing and exercising a deep-rooted sexism (which, again, had been exulted as positive during the Reagan era). Mason highlights how Lyman objectifies those women and he takes the concept not only as an expression of private yearnings, but as driven by a society that widely endorses such behaviour. In times like ours, a perspective that unites a critique of capitalism as connected to gender and its political implications, stands out as one that must be considered.

Another thought-provoking look on the play comes from Abbotson who suggests linking the figure of Lyman Felt to that of his forerunner, Willy Loman (from *Death of a Salesman*), therefore bringing to the surface the forces that determine these two iconic characters. She points out the fact that 'Both are salesmen, selling the materialistic U.S. dream of wealth and success by denying certain aspects of reality'. Both also buttress the glories of the self-made man who should pursue the American Dream, even though Lyman is a figure that achieved it while Loman was defeated by it. In their attempt to guide their demeanour towards the realization of the Dream, both lives have come out more like a nightmare. In another study, Abbotson also explores the symbolism and power of the characters' names, revealing and signalizing their conditions. Miller has insisted he named Loman after a scene he saw in the film *The Testament of Dr. Mabuse* where a detective is duped, reduced to terror and ends calling the name 'Lohmann?' into a phone. For Miller this name signified 'a terrified man calling into the void for help that will never come.' However, as Abbotson suggests, 'Loman's name tends to evoke discussion of Willy Loman as a 'low man' in terms of his abilities, character or prospects' and to the larger society Willy is certainly viewed as inferior, disposable and small, despite his willingness to kill himself to get the insurance money for his family. Lyman, on the other hand, is a 'lie man' who deceives people for his own advantage and pleasure while (ironically) having an insurance company. The choice of the characters' names in Miller's plays provides a comment on their background, characterization or even their destiny, and this is also a great source for wider study.

Behind the scenes – interview with David Esbjornson who directed *The Ride Down Mt. Morgan* at the Public Theater in 1998 and on Broadway in 2000

His experience on meeting Miller

I was trying to find my relationship to the play and to some extent to Arthur which was a completely new relationship. When I met him it was so humbling. I could understand why he was such a big celebrity. I was really surprised that from the moment we sat down, he was interested in what I had to say.

Working with Miller and how the script was altered

Arthur's work was under a kind of scrutiny. There were some criticisms of how he portrayed women, in particular. So what I attempt to do (and this is true in Shakespeare as well), where women are not presented as dimensionally as the men are, I want to determine what their circumstances are, why they are motivated to do what they do, and often-times, you'll find a very credible and interesting story to tell. An example: we needed to inform that Leah was pregnant, but showing her manipulating Lyman to get married by threatening abortion seemed to undermine both Leah and the moral balance of the play. Lyman could easily run away from responsibility for his own actions. Lyman's decision to undertake two marriages was his own, not some 'evil woman's' trick, and I felt compelled to make a change if he were to allow it. I felt obligated to clarify that for my own generation as well as to his. Because something like that can undermine the play if it isn't dealt with.

I also suggested we cut off a scene in which there was Raoul, Lyman's business partner. When Miller saw it in the first preview at the Public he came to me and said: 'We don't need that scene, do we?' The play moves back and forth in time, so it could be very confusing if we weren't really sharp and clear about where you were and when it was. Even if you are in the fantasy, you need to understand how it fits into the whole. I remember having this idea that all the interns at the hospital would turn into giant crows and tear Lyman's entrails out, and that would be one of his bad dream fantasies. I thought Arthur would think all that was crazy, some kind of conceptual overreach. But, he paused for a minute and said: 'That sounds like a really good idea'. Still, I always wanted to make sure that when we went to those absurd places that we would come back and grab hold of the narrative again.

On changes between public and Broadway productions

The production had expanded some. There were more shifts in time, and acting moments. I embellished the staging and gave it a sharper choreography. I think everything went kind of up a notch in its presentation. The floating hospital curtains flowed better, the clothes were more expensive, and there were fur coats which gave a stronger sense of the upper middle class life. Some things we just couldn't afford to do off-Broadway.

On 1980s Reaganism

The play is about an era of privilege of excess, where certain people felt as though they are impervious to all the other struggles that are going on. AIDS, for example. Lyman's attitudes, his ego, are all aspects of this kind of new American attitude – 'Do it the way you want, don't let anybody tell you differently' and 'Let everyone else play by the rules'. We have this Wild West cowboy thing, that we must fight for our individual wants and desires, take it to the edge, see what happens. There is a strange self-destructiveness there. I asked Arthur, 'Do you think Lyman wanted to kill himself?' And he told me 'I don't know if he knew. He was going to push the circumstances as far as he could and let fate determine the outcome'.

Tragedy, comedy, or a balance between the two?

The first scene of the play is almost a situation comedy, but I kept a kind of darkness in my production. In the opening of the play, it's snowing. And, the snow revealed multiple fragmented images. The nurse floated across the top of the set in her chair, there is a bed hovering in the air, and when a member of the 'ski patrol' moving in a slow-motion search, reaches the accident, the bed just blows apart and we find ourselves with Lyman in the hospital. This was all established before we got to the first scene.

Play's contemporary relevance

Currently folks are looking at other things. They may not be as interested in the people or some of the concerns of upper, white, middle class, first world problems. But I think Arthur still deals with a lot of interesting ideas in this play: working women and kids, infidelity, marriage, cultural hypocrisy and death. And in addition to the fun of the wild plot, different timelines and fantasies going back and forth, I think Arthur was trying to write honestly about his character and perhaps himself. What does it mean to approach life in such a bold and selfish way? Arthur always manages to give us something to unpack and think about.

In that way, the play has a future and it might be something people will want to re-visit.

Further study

Abbotson, Susan C. W. 'From Loman to Lyman: The Salesman Forty Years On'. *'The Salesman Has a Birthday': Essays Celebrating the Fiftieth Anniversary of Arthur Miller's Death of a Salesman*, edited by Steve Marino. University Press of America, 2000, pp. 99–108

Explores the play by contextualizing it in relation to *Death of a Salesman* and sheds light on many relevant aspects that also point out to the social forces that shape the play by diving into the concept of the American Dream and its effects.

Bigsby, Christopher. *'The Ride down Mount Morgan'*. *Arthur Miller: A Critical Study.* Cambridge University Press, 2005, pp. 366–380

Arthur Miller's biographer brings in a broad range of aspects and draws our attention to the cultural landscape of the United States in the 1980s and how the play relates to this. He also shares responses to the play when performed in London and in the United States.

Centola, Steven R. '"How to Contain the Impulse of Betrayal": A Sartrean Reading of *The Ride down Mount Morgan'*. *American Drama* 6, no. 1, Fall 1996, pp. 14–28.

This reading promotes an interesting and intense discussion about Sartre's conception of freedom and its implications. Some scholars have explored the philosophical/existentialist gist of the play, but few have reached Centola's depth.

Mason, Jeffrey D. 'The Women'. *Stone Tower: The Political Theater of Arthur Miller.* University of Michigan Press, 2011, pp. 205–259

The author has one of the sharpest critiques of gender, discrimination, exploitation and other political topics that frame Miller's plays as connected to capitalism. He widely explores Lyman's sexism towards the women in this study.

Russo, Thiago. '*Reaganism in* The Ride Down Mt. Morgan.' *Arthur Miller for the Twenty-First Century: Contemporary Views of His Writings and Ideas,* edited by Stephen Marino and David Palmer. Palgrave Macmillan, 2020, pp. 197–210

This study was written with a fierce look on the political and economic forces that shaped both the plot and the form of the play. Presenting a critique of the Reagan era, this study was based on a PhD thesis that was elected the best in the English programme, of Humanities (USP) in Brazil, and is running for best thesis of the country at CAPES award.

Woods, Alan. 'Consuming the Past: Commercial American Theatre in the Reagan Era'. *The American Stage: Social and Economic Issues from the Colonial Period to the Present*, **edited by Ron Engle and Tice L. Miller. Cambridge University Press, 1993, pp. 252–66**

The author has a keen eye as to how the conservative ideology of the 1980s was materialized in some plays of the 1980/90s in the United States, presenting figures, plots and reviews of that period, giving the reader a sense of what the country was experiencing as opposed to what it was showing in the theatre venues.

The Ride Down Mt. Morgan

The play follows Lyman Felt's mind through scenes in real time as well as in memory and dream. The set must therefore be an open one to allow scenes to move fluidly without pause excepting as noted in the text.

Lyman can leave and enter the hospital bed without having to change in and out of costumes; simply by his drawing covers up near his chin, even though dressed, it is sufficient to suggest him in a hospital gown. Where indicated, however, he should be in a gown.

This final acting version reflects the David Esbjornson production at the Public Theater, New York, in the Fall of 1998.

The Characters

Lyman Felt
Theo Felt
Leah Felt
Bessie
Nurse Logan
Tom Wilson

Act One

Scene One

Lyman Felt *asleep in a hospital bed.*

Nurse Logan *is reading a magazine in a chair a few feet away. She is black. He is deeply asleep, snoring now and then.*

Lyman (*his eyes still shut*)   Thank you, thank you all very much. Please be seated. (**Nurse** *turns, looks toward him.*) We have a lot of . . . not material . . . yes, material . . . to cover this afternoon, so please take your seats and cross your . . . No-no . . . (*Laughs weakly.*) . . . Not cross your legs, just take your seats. . . .

Nurse   That was a lot of surgery, Mr. Felt. You're supposed to be resting . . . Or you out?

Lyman (*for a moment he sleeps, snores, then*)   . . . Today I would like you to consider life insurance from a different perspective. I want you to look at the whole economic system as one enormous tit. (**Nurse** *chuckles quietly.*) So the job of the individual is to get a good place in line for a suck. (*She laughs louder.*) Which gives us the word 'suckcess'. Or . . . or not.

Nurse   You know, you better settle down after all that surgery.

Lyman (*opens his eyes*)   You black?

Nurse   That's what they keep telling me.

Lyman   Good for you. I've got the biggest training program of any company for you guys. And the first one that ever put them in sales. There's no election now, is there? —Eisenhower or something?

Nurse   It's December. And he's been dead since I don't know when.

Lyman   Eisenhower *dead?* (*Peers in confusion.*) Oh, right, right! . . . Why can't I move, do you mind?

Nurse (*returns to her chair*)   You're all in a cast, you broke a lot of bones.

Lyman   Who?

Nurse   You. You smashed your car. They say you went skiing down that Mount Morgan in a Porsche.

She chuckles. He squints, trying to orient himself.

Lyman   Where . . . where . . . I'm where?

Nurse   Clearhaven Memorial Hospital.

Lyman   That Earl Hines?

Nurse   Who?

Lyman   That piano. Sounds like Earl Hines. (*Sings an Earl Hines tune. Laughs appreciatively.*) Listen to that, will you? That beautiful? Jimmy Baldwin . . . long, long ago when I was still a writer . . . used to say, 'Lyman, you're a nigger underneath.' (*Chuckles; it fades. Now with some anxiety.*) . . . Where?

Nurse   Clearhaven Memorial Hospital.

Lyman (*it is slowly penetrating*)   *Clearhaven?*

Nurse   Your wife and daughter just arrived up from New York. They're out in the visitors' room.

Lyman (*canniness attempt, but still confused*)   . . . From *New York?* Why? Who called them?

Nurse   What do you mean? Why not?

Lyman   And where is this?

Nurse   Clearhaven.—I'm from Canada myself, I only just started here. We've still got railroads in Canada.

Lyman (*a moment of silent confusion*)   Listen. I'm not feeling well . . . why are we talking about Canadian railroads?

Nurse   No, I just mentioned it, as there is a storm.

Lyman   Now what . . . what . . . what was that about my wife . . . New York?

Nurse   She's here in the waiting room . . .

Lyman   Here in the waiting . . .

Nurse   . . . And your daughter.

Lyman (*tension rising with clearing of mind; he looks at his hands, turns them over*)   . . . Would you mind?—Just . . . touch me? (*She touches his face; he angers with the fully dawning fact.*) Who the hell called them, for God's sake? Why didn't somebody ask me?

Nurse   I'm new here! I'm sorry if I'm not satisfactory.

Lyman (*high anxiety*)   Who said you're not satisfactory? What is this . . . endless *verbiage?*—not verbiage, for Christ's sake, I meant . . . (*Panting.*) Listen, I absolutely can't see anyone and they have to go back to New York right away.

Nurse   But as long as you're awake . . .

Lyman   Immediately! Go—get them out of here! (*A jab of pain.*) Ow!—Please, quickly, go!—Wait!—There's no . . . like another . . . you know, woman out there?

Nurse   Not while I was out there.

Lyman   Please . . . quickly, huh? I can't see anybody. (*Bewildered,* **Nurse** *exits*). Oh, poor Theo—here! My God, what have I done! How could I have gone out on that road in a storm! (*Terrified of self-betrayal.*) Have you lost your fucking mind?! (*Frozen in anguish, he stares straight ahead as music is heard. His mood changes as he is caught by his catastrophic vision.*) Oh, dear God, this mustn't happen.

His wife, **Theo**, *and daughter,* **Bessie**, *are discovered seated on a waiting room settee. A burst of weeping from* **Bessie**. *He is not looking directly at them but imagining them.*

Oh, Bessie, my poor Bessie! (*Covers his eyes, as* **Bessie** *weeps.*) No-no-no, it mustn't happen!—think of something else!—

His vision is forcing him out of the bed in his hospital gown. Music fades out.

Theo (*touching* **Bessie**'s *hand*)   Darling, try not to.

Bessie   I can't help it.

Theo   Of course you can. Be brave now, dear.

Lyman (*moving into the range of the women*)   Oh yes! My Theo! That's exactly what she'd say! What a woman!

Theo   Try to think of all the happiness; think of his laughter; Daddy loves life, he'll fight for it.

Bessie   . . . I guess I've just never had anything really bad happen.

Lyman (*a few feet away*)   Oh, my dear child . . . !

Theo   But you'll see as you get older—everything ultimately fits together . . . and for the good.

Lyman (*staring front*)   Oh yes . . . good old Episcopal Theo!

Theo   —Now come, Bessie.—Remember what a wonderful time we had in Africa? Think of Africa.

Bessie   What an amazing woman you are, Mother.

Nurse Logan *enters.*

Nurse   It'll still be a while before he can see anybody. Would you like me to call a motel? It's ski season, but my husband can probably get you in, he plows their driveway.

Bessie   Do you know if he's out of danger?

Nurse   I'm sure the doctors will let you know. (*Obviously changing the subject.*) I can't believe you made it up from New York in this sleet.

Theo   One does what one has to. Actually . . . would you mind calling the motel? It was a terrible drive . . .

Nurse   Sometimes I feel like going back to Canada—at least we had a railroad.

Theo   We'll have them again; things take time in this country but in the end we get them done.

Nurse   Don't hesitate if you want more tea.

Nurse *exits*.

Theo (*turns to* **Bessie**, *smiling painfully*)   Why'd you start to laugh?

Bessie (*touching* **Theo**'s *hand*)   It's nothing . . .

Theo   Well, what is it?

Bessie   Well . . . I mean things really don't always get done in this country.

Theo (*disengaging her hand; she is hurt*)   I think they do, ultimately. I've lived through changes that were inconceivable thirty years ago. (*Straining to laugh*.) Really, dear, I'm not *that* naive.

Bessie (*angering*)   Well, don't be upset!—They certainly are very nice people around here, aren't they?

Theo (*managing to pull her mood together*)   I'm sorry you never knew small town life—there is a goodness.

Bessie   I'm wondering if we should call Grandma Esther.

Theo (*dutifully*)   If you like. (*Slight pause.* **Bessie** *is still.*) She gets so impressively emotional, that's all. But call . . . she *is* his mother.

Bessie   I know she's a superficial woman, but I can't help it, I . . .

Theo   But you *should* like her, she adores you; she simply never liked me and I've always known it, that's all. (*She looks away*.)

Bessie   I mean she can be awfully funny sometimes. And she *is* warm.

Theo   Warm? Yes, I suppose—provided it doesn't commit her to anything or anyone. I've never hidden it, dear—I think she's the center of his psychological problem . . .

Lyman   Perfect!

Theo   . . . But I suppose I'm prejudiced.

Lyman *laughs silently with a head shake of joyful recognition.*

I used to think it was because he didn't marry Jewish, but . . .

Bessie   But she didn't either.

Theo   Darling, she'd have disliked any woman he married . . . except an heiress or a sexpot. But go ahead, I do think you should call her. (**Bessie** *stands.*) And give her my love, will you?

Lyman *issues a cackling laugh of appreciation of her nature.*

Leah *enters. She is in her thirties; in an open raccoon coat, high heels.* **Nurse** *enters with her.*

Lyman (*on the instant she enters, claps his hands over his eyes*)   No, she mustn't! It can't happen! She mustn't! (*Unable to bear it, he starts to flee, but stops as . . .*)

Leah   After all the money we've put into this hospital it seems to me I ought to be able to speak to the chief nurse, for Christ's sake!

Nurse   I'm doing my best to get her for you . . . !

Leah   Well hurry, will you? (**Nurse** *starts to exit.*) I'm only asking for a little information, dear!

Nurse *exits. Pause.*

Lyman (*imploring himself, his eyes clamped shut*)   Think of something else. Let's see now—the new Mercedes convertible . . . that actress, what's her name . . . ? (*But he fails to escape; and scared, slowly turns his head toward . . .*)

Leah, *who sits, but quickly stands again and moves restlessly.* **Theo** *and* **Bessie** *observe her indirectly, with polite curiosity. Now their eyes meet.* **Leah** *throws up her hands.*

Leah   The same thing when I had my baby here, it was like pulling teeth to get them to tell me if it was a boy or a girl.

Bessie   Is it an emergency?

Leah   Yes, my husband; he cracked up the car on Mount Morgan. You?

Bessie   My father. It was a car, too.

Lyman (*eyes heavenward, hands clasped*)   Oh please, please!

Theo   The roads are impossible.

Leah   I can't imagine what got into him, driving down Mount Morgan on ice . . . and at night yet! It's incomprehensible! (*A sudden explosion.*) Damn them, I have a right to know what's happening! (*She charges out.*)

Bessie   Poor thing.

Theo   But she *knows* how busy they are . . .

Silence now; **Theo** *leans back, closing her eyes. Another sobbing fit threatens* **Bessie***, who downs it, covers her eyes. Then suddenly she breaks down and weeps.*

Oh Bessie, dear, try not to.

Bessie (*shaking her head helplessly*)   . . . I just love him so!

Leah *returns, more subdued now. She sits tiredly, closes her eyes. Pause. She gets up, goes to a window, looks out.*

Leah   *Now* the moon comes out!—everybody smashes up in the dark and now you could read a paper out there.

Bessie   You live around here?

Leah   Not far. We're out near the lake.

Bessie   It looks like beautiful country.

Leah   Oh, it is. But I'll take New York anytime. (*A great sob suddenly bursts from her; she chokes it back.*) I'm sorry. (*But she weeps again, helplessly into her handkerchief.* **Bessie** *is affected and begins weeping, too.*)

Theo   Now really . . . ! (*Shakes* **Bessie**'*s arm.*) Stop this! (*She sees* **Leah**'*s indignant look.*) You still don't know how serious it is, why do you carry on like this?

Leah, (*rather unwillingly*) You're probably right.

Theo (*exulting—to* **Bessie** *as well*) Of course! I mean there's always time to despair, why should . . . ?

Leah (*sharply*) I *said* you were right, I was agreeing with you! (**Theo** *turns away stiffly.*) I'm sorry.

Now the women go motionless.

Lyman (*marveling*) What strong, admirable women they are! What definite characters! Thank God I'm only imagining this to torture myself . . . But it's enough! (*Starts resolutely toward the bed, but caught by his vision, halts.*) Now what would they say next?

The women reanimate.

Bessie You raise things on your place?

Leah We grow most of what we eat. And we're starting to raise a few thoroughbreds now, in a small way.

Bessie Oh, I'd love that . . .

Leah I envy your composure—both of you. Really, you make me feel better. What part of New York are you in?

Bessie East Seventy-fourth Street.

Lyman Oh no! No no!

Leah Really! We often stay at the Carlyle . . .

Bessie Oh, it's practically around the corner.

Theo You sound like a New Yorker.

Leah I went to NYU School of Business for three years; I loved it but I was raised up here in Elmira . . . and my business is here, so . . .

Theo What sort of business do you have?

Leah Insurance.

Bessie That's what Daddy does!

Lyman (*knocking his knuckles against his head*) No-no-no-no-no!

Leah   Well, there's a million of us. You in it too?

Bessie   No, I'm at home . . . take care of my husband.

Leah   I'm hoping to sell out in a couple of years, get a place in Manhattan somewhere, and just paint morning to night the rest of my life.

Bessie   Really! My husband's a painter.

Leah   Professionally, or . . . ?

Bessie   Oh yes. He's Harold Lamb.

Lyman *rushes over to the bed and pulls the covers over his head.*

Leah   Harold Lamb?

Leah (*ceases all movement, staring at* **Bessie***. She turns to stare at* **Theo***.*)

Theo   What is it?

Leah   Your husband is really Harold Lamb?

Bessie (*very pleased and proud*)   You've heard of him?

Leah   You're not Mrs. Felt, are you?

Theo   Why yes.

Leah (*her puzzled look*)   Then you . . . (*Breaks off, then . . .*) You're not here for Lyman, are you?

Bessie   You know Daddy?

Leah   But . . . (*Turning from one to the other . . .*) how'd they come to notify *you?*

Lyman (*sits up in bed and raises a devout, monitory hand to heaven, whispering loudly*)   Stop it, stop it, stop it . . . !

Theo (*uncomprehending, but beginning to take affront*)   Why shouldn't they notify me?

Leah   Well . . . after so many years.

Theo   What do you mean?

Leah   But it's over nine . . .

Theo   What is?

Leah   Your divorce.

Theo *and* **Bessie** *are struck dumb. A silence.*

You're Theodora Felt, right?

Theo   Who *are* you?

Leah   I'm Leah. Leah Felt.

Theo (*a haughtiness begins*)   Felt!

Leah   Lyman is my husband.

Theo   Who *are* you? What are you talking about!

Bessie (*intensely curious about* **Leah**, *she angers at* **Theo**)   Well don't get *angry,* for heaven's sake!

Theo   Be quiet!

Leah (*seeing* **Theo**'*s genuineness*)   Well, you're divorced, aren't you?

Theo   Divorced!—who the hell *are* you!

Leah   I'm Lyman's wife. (**Theo** *sees she is a serious woman; it silences her.*)

Bessie   When . . . when did you . . . ? I mean . . .

Theo (*in motion again*)   She's insane!—she's some kind of a nut!

Leah (*to* **Bessie**)   It was nine years this past July.

Theo   Really. And who performed this . . . this *event?*

Leah   The Reno City Hall clerk, later a rabbi here in Elmira. My son's name is Benjamin, for Lyman's father, and Alexander for his great-grandmother—Benjamin Alexander Felt.

Theo (*with a weak attempt to sustain mockery*)   Really!

Leah   Yes, I'm terribly sorry if you didn't know.

Theo   Didn't know *what?* What are you *talking* about?

Leah   We have been married a little over nine years, Mrs. Felt.

Theo   Have you? And I suppose you have some document . . . ?

Leah   I have our marriage certificate, I guess . . .

Theo   You guess!

Leah (*angrily*)   Well I'm sure I do! And I know I have Lyman's will in our safe deposit box . . .

Theo (*helplessly mocking*)   And it names you as his wife!

Leah   And Benjamin as his son. (**Theo** *is halted by her factuality.*) . . . But I guess you have more or less the same . . . is that right? (**Theo** *is still as a stone.*) There really was no divorce?

Bessie (*with a glance at her stricken mother . . . softly, almost apologetically*)   . . . No.

Leah   Well, I guess we'd better . . . meet, or something. And talk. (**Theo** *is staring into space.*) Mrs. Felt? I understand your feelings, but you'll just have to believe it, I guess—we have a terrible problem. Mrs. Felt?

Theo   It's impossible, nine years ago . . . (*To* **Bessie***:*) That's when we all went to Africa.

Bessie   Oh, right!—the safari!

Theo (*to* **Leah**, *with a victorious, if nearly demented laugh.*)   We were never closer in our lives! We traveled through Kenya, Nigeria . . . (*As though this clinched everything.*) . . . we even flew to Egypt!

Nurse *enters. It instantly galvanizes all of them. She glances from one to the other.*

Nurse   Doctor Lowry would like to see Mrs. Felt now.

For one instant no one moves—then both **Theo** *and* **Leah** *rise simultaneously. This actualization of* **Leah***'s claim stiffens* **Theo**, *forcing her to start assertively toward the* **Nurse**—*and she sways and starts to fall to the floor.*

Leah   Catch her!

Bessie   Mother!

Nurse *and* **Bessie** *catch* **Theo**, *then lower her to the floor.*

Leah (*over her shoulder*)   Help here, someone's fainted! Where the hell is a doctor, goddammit! (*To the air:*) Is there a doctor in this fucking hospital?!

Blackout.

Scene Two

A couch and chair. **Leah** *is seated facing* **Tom Wilson**, *a middle-aged but very fit lawyer who is reading a will, and sipping coffee. After a moment she gets up and moves to a point and stares, eyes filled with fear. Then dialing a cell phone, turns to him.*

Leah   Sure you wouldn't like some toast?—Sorry I'm not being much of a hostess.

Tom (*immersed*)   Thanks. I'm just about done here.

Leah (*dialing*)   God, I dread it—my boy'll be home any minute . . . (*Into phone:*) Put my brother on, Tina. . . . Lou?—I don't know, they won't let me see him yet. What'd Uniroyal say? *What?* Well get on it, will you, call L.A. this minute! I mean for God's sake, Lou, I want that business! (*Hangs up.*) How much do you have to pay relatives to get them to do any work? (**Tom** *closes the file, turns to her, silent.*)—I know you're her lawyer, but I'm not really asking advice, am I?

Tom   I can discuss this. (*Returns her file.*) The will does recognize the boy as his son, but you are not his wife.

Leah (*lifting the file*)   Even if this refers to me as his wife?

Tom   I'm afraid that's legally meaningless, since he never divorced. However . . . (*Breaks off, pressing his eyes.*) I'm just stunned, I simply can't absorb it.

Leah   I'm still in midair someplace.

Tom   What'd you ask me? Oh yes—provided the legal wife gets a minimum of one third of the estate he can leave you as much as he likes. So you're very well taken care of. (*Sighs, leaning forward and gripping his head.*) He actually flies a plane, you say?

Leah   Oh yes, soaring planes, too.

Tom   You know, for years he'd never get off the ground unless it was unavoidable.

Leah   Oh, he's wonderful in the air. (*Pause.*) I'm not here. I'm simply . . . not here. Can he be two people? Is that possible?

Tom   . . . May I ask you . . . ?

Leah   Please. . . . Incidentally, have you known him long?

Tom   Sixteen, seventeen years.—When you decided to marry, I assume he told you he'd gotten a divorce . . .

Leah   Of course. We went to Reno together.

Tom   No kidding! And what happened?

Leah   God, I'd forgotten all about this . . . (*Breaks off.*) How could I be so *stupid!* —You see, it was July, streets were boiling hot, so he had me stay in the hotel while he went to pick up his divorce decree . . . (*She goes silent.*)

Tom   Yes?

Leah (*shaking her head*)   God!—my gullibility!—I was curious to see what a decree looked like, so . . .

Lyman *enters, wearing a short-sleeved summer shirt and cowboy hat.*

No particular reason, but I'd never seen one . . .

Lyman   I threw it away.

Leah (*with a surprised laugh*)   Why!

Lyman   I don't want to look back, I feel twenty-five! (*Laughs.*) You look stunned!

Leah   I guess I never believed you'd marry me, darling.

Lyman (*he draws her to him*)   Feeling is all I really believe in, Leah—you're making me see that again. Feeling is chaos, but any decent thing I've ever done was out of feeling, and every lousy thing I'm ashamed of came from careful thinking. I simply can't lose you, Leah, you're precious to me.—You look scared . . . what is it?

Leah   I don't want to say it.

Lyman   Go ahead. Please!

Leah   Every relationship I've known gets to where it needs a lie to keep it going.

Lyman   But does that always have to be!

Leah (*hesitates*)   Can I say something? I wish we could make a different wedding vow; like 'Dearly beloved, I promise everything good, but I might have to lie to you sometimes.' (*He is taken aback, but grins.*) —I wanted to say that, okay? You're shocked, aren't you.

Lyman   What balls you have to say that! —Come here. (*Takes her hand, closes his eyes.*) I'm going to learn to fly a plane.

Leah   What are you talking about?

Lyman   Because flying terrifies me. I'm going to wrestle down one fear at a time till I've dumped them all and I am a free man! (*Gripping her hands, nose to nose.*) I have a car and driver downstairs. (*Holds out his beckoning arm.*) Come to your wedding, Leah, my darling!

Lyman *exits without lowering his arm.*

Leah   . . . And it was all lies! How is it possible! Why did he do it? What did he want?

Tom   Actually, though . . . (*Tries to recall.*) Yes, I think it was about nine years ago, we did have a discussion about a divorce . . . although at the time I didn't take it all that seriously. He suddenly popped in one day with this "research" he said he'd done . . .

Lyman *enters in a business suit.* **Tom** *has moved out of* **Leah***'s area.*

Lyman   . . . I've been looking into bigamy, Tom.

Tom (*laughs, surprised*)   Bigamy!—what are you talking about?

Lyman   You know there's an enormous amount of it in the United States now.

Tom   Really? But what's the point . . . ?

Lyman   . . . And not just among blacks or the poor. I've been wondering about a desertion insurance policy. Might call it the Bigamy Protection Plan. (**Tom** *laughs.*) I'm serious. We could set the premiums really low. Be great, especially for minority women.

Tom (*admiringly*)   Say now! Where the hell do you get these ideas?

Lyman   Just put myself in other people's places. —Incidentally, how frequently do they prosecute for bigamy anymore, you have any idea?

Tom   None whatsoever. But it's a victimless crime so it can't be often.

Lyman   That's my impression, too. Get somebody to research it, will you, I want to be sure. —I'll be in Elmira till Friday. (**Lyman** *starts to leave but dawdles.*)

Tom   Why do I think you're depressed?

Lyman   . . . I guess I am—slightly. (*The grin.*) I'm turning fifty-four this July.

Tom   Fifty's much tougher, I think.

Lyman   My father died at fifty-three.

Tom   Well, you're over the hump. Anyway, you're in better shape than anybody I know.

Lyman   Famous last words.

Tom   Something wrong, Lyman?

Lyman   I don't think I have the balls. (*A laugh. Moves into high tension; then, facing his challenge, turns rather abruptly to* **Tom**.)

There's no man I trust like you, Tom. (*A grin.*) —I guess you know I've cheated on Theodora.

Tom   Well, I've had my suspicions, yes—ever since I walked in on you humping that Pakistani typist on your desk.

Lyman (*laughs*)   'Humping!' —I love that Presbyterian jive of yours, haven't heard that in years.

Tom   Quaker.

Lyman (*confessionally, quietly*)   There've been more than that one, Tommy.

Tom (*laughs*)   God, where do you get the time?

Lyman   Disgust you?

Tom   Not catastrophically.

Lyman (*pause; he composes himself, then . . . again with the grin*)   I think I've fallen in love.

Tom   Oh Lyman . . . don't tell me!

Lyman (*pointing at him and laughing nervously*)   Look at you!— God, you really love Theodora, don't you!

Tom   Of course I do!—you're not thinking of divorce, are you?

Lyman   I don't know. Maybe I just wanted to say it aloud to somebody.

Tom   But how sure are you about your feelings for this woman?

Lyman   I'm sure. A new woman has always been an undiscovered shore, but I'd really like to go straight now, Tom. I want one woman for the rest of my life. And I can't quite see it being Theodora.

Tom   You know she loves you deeply, Lyman.

Lyman   Tom, I love her, too. But after thirty-two years we bore each other, we just do. And boredom is a form of deception, isn't it. And deception has become like my Nazi, my worst horror—I want nothing now but to wear my own face on my face every day till the day I die. Or do you think that kind of honesty is possible?

Tom   I don't have to tell you, the problem is not honesty but how much you hurt others with it.

Lyman   Right. What about your religion? But there's no solution there either, I guess.

Tom   I somehow can't imagine you praying, Lyman. (*Short pause.*)

Lyman   Is there an answer?

Tom   I don't know, maybe all one can do is hope to end up with the right regrets.

Lyman   You ever cheated, Tom?

Tom   No.

Lyman   Honest to God?—I've seen you eye the girls around here.

Tom   It's the truth.

Lyman   Is that the regret you end up with?

Tom *laughs bashfully, then* **Lyman** *joins him. And suddenly,* **Lyman***'s embarrassment and suffering are on his face.*

. . . Shit, that was cruel, Tom, forgive me, will you? Dammit, why do I let myself get depressed? It's all pointless guilt, that's all! Here I start from nothing, create forty-two hundred jobs for people and raise over sixty ghetto blacks to office positions when that was not easy to do—I should be proud of myself, son of a bitch! And I am! I am! (*He bangs on the desk, then subsides, looks front and downward.*) I love your view. That red river of taillights gliding down Park Avenue on a winter's night—and all those silky white thighs crossing inside those heated limousines . . . Christ, can there be a sexier vision in the world? (*Turning back to* **Tom**.) I keep thinking of my father—how connected he was to his life; couldn't wait to open the store every morning and happily count the pickles, rearrange the olive barrels. People like that knew the main thing. Which is what? What is the main thing, do you know?

Tom *is silent.*

—Look, don't worry, I really can't imagine myself without Theodora, she's a great, great wife! . . . I love that woman! It's always good talking to you, Tom. (*Starts to go, halts.*) Maybe it's simply that if you try to live according to your real desires, you have to end up looking like a shit.

Lyman *exits.* **Leah** *covers her face and there is a pause as* **Tom** *observes her.*

Tom   I'm sorry.

Leah   He had it all carefully worked out from the very beginning.

Tom   I'd say it was more like . . . a continuous improvisation.

Leah   It was the baby, you see—once I was pregnant he simply wouldn't listen to reason . . .

Lyman *hurries on in a winter overcoat, claps a hand over her mouth.*

Lyman   Don't tell me it's too late. (*Kisses her.*) Did you do it?

Leah   I was just walking out the door for the hospital.

Lyman   Oh, thank God. (*Draws her to a seat, and pulls her down.*) Please, dear, give me one full minute and then you can do as you like.

Leah (*with pain*)   Don't, Lyme, it's impossible.

Lyman   You know if you do this it's going to change it between us.

Leah   Darling, it comes down to being a single parent and I just don't want that.

Lyman   I've already named him.

Leah (*amused, touching his face*)   How do you know it's a him?

Lyman   I'm never wrong. I have a very intimate relationship with ladies' bellies. His name is Benjamin after my father and Alexander after my mother's mother, who I loved a lot. (*Grins at his own egoism.*) You can put in a middle name.

Leah (*with an unhappy laugh*)   Well thanks so much! (*She tries to stand up but he holds her.*) He asked me not to be late.

Lyman   The Russians—this is an ancient custom—before an important parting, they sit for a moment in silence. Give Benjamin this moment.

Leah   He's not Benjamin, now stop it!

Lyman   Believe in your feelings, Leah, the rest is nonsense. What do you really and truly want?

Silence for a moment.

I would drive him to school in the mornings and take him to ball games.

Leah   Twice a month?

Lyman   With the new office set up here, I could easily be with you more than half the time.

Leah   And Theodora?

Lyman   It's difficult to talk about her.

Leah   With me, you mean?

Lyman   I can't lie to myself, darling, she's been a tremendous wife. It would be too unjust.

Leah   But keeping it a secret—where does that leave me? It's hard enough to identify myself as it is. And I can't believe she won't find out sooner or later, and then what?

Lyman   If I actually have to choose it'll be you. But she doesn't know a soul in this whole area, it'd be a million-to-one shot for her to ever find out. I'm practically with you half the time now, and it's been pretty good, hasn't it?

Leah (*touching her belly*)   . . . But what do we tell this? . . .

Lyman   . . . Benjamin.

Leah   Oh stop calling him Benjamin! It's not even three weeks!

Lyman   That's long enough to be Benjamin—he has a horoscope, stars and planets; he has a *future!*

Leah   . . . Why do I feel we're circling around something? There's something I don't believe here—what is it?

Lyman   Maybe that I'm this desperate. (*Kisses her belly.*)

Leah   Are you? —I can't express it . . . there's just something about this baby that doesn't seem . . . I don't know—inevitable.

Lyman   Darling, I haven't wanted anything this much since my twenties, when I was struggling to be a poet and make something of my own that would last.

Leah   Really.

Lyman   It's the truth.

Leah   That's touching, Lyman, I'm very moved.

So it is up in the air for a moment.

But I can't, I won't, it's the story of my life, I always end up with all the responsibility; I'd have to be in total charge of your child and I know I'd resent it finally—and maybe even you as well. You're putting me back to being twelve or thirteen and my parents asking *me* where to go on vacation, or what kind of car to buy or what color drapes. I hate that position! One of the most sensuous things about you was that I could lie back and let you drive, and now you're putting me behind the wheel again. It's just all wrong.

Lyman   I thought if we lived together let's say ten years, you'd still be in the prime, and pretty rich, and I'd . . .

Leah   . . . Walk away into the sunset.

Lyman   I'm trying to be as cruelly realistic as life, darling. Have you ever loved a man the way you love me?

Leah   No.

Lyman   Well? That's the only reality.

Leah   You can drive me to the hospital, if you like realism so much. (*She stands; he does.*) You look so sad! You poor man.

She kisses him; a silent farewell is in the kiss; she gets her coat and turns to him.

I won't weaken on this, dear, so make up your mind.

Lyman We're going to lose each other if you do this. I feel it.

Leah Well, there's a very simple way not to lose me, dear, I guess that's why they invented it.—Come, wait in the hospital if you want to. If not, I'll be back tomorrow. (*She draws him on, but he halts.*)

Lyman Will you give me a week to tell her? It's still early for you, isn't it?

Leah Tell her what?

Lyman . . . That I'm going to marry you.

Tom I see.

Lyman *moves into darkness.*

Leah I don't understand it; he'd had dozens of women, why did he pick me to be irreplaceable? (*She looks down at her watch, stares in silence.*) God! How do I tell my boy?

Tom He's nine now?

Leah And worships Lyman. Worships him.

Tom I'd better get to the hospital. (*He moves to go, halts hesitantly.*) Don't answer this if you'd rather not, but you think you could ever take him back?

Leah (*thinks for a moment*)   How could you ask me that? It's outrageous!—Would Theodora? She struck me as a rather judgmental sort of woman.

Tom Oh, she has a tender side, too.—I guess she hasn't had time to think of the future, any more than you have.

Leah All this reminds me of an idea I used to have about him that . . . well, it'll sound mystical and silly . . .

Tom Please. I'd love to understand him.

Leah   Well, it's just that he wants so much; like a kid at a fair; a jelly apple here, a cotton candy there, and then a ride on a loop-the-loop . . . and it never lets up in him; it's what's so attractive about him—to women, I mean—Lyman's mind is up your skirt but it's such a rare thing to be wanted like that—indifference is what most men feel now—I mean they have an appetite but not hunger—and here is such a splendidly hungry man and it's simply . . . well . . . precious once you're past twenty-five. I tell you the truth, somewhere deep down I think I sensed something about him wasn't on the level, but . . . I guess I must have loved him so much that I . . . (*Breaks off.*)—But I mustn't talk this way; he's unforgivable! It's the rottenest thing I've ever heard of! The answer is no, absolutely not!

Tom (*nods, thinks, then . . .*)   Well, I'll be off. I hope it's not too difficult for you with the little boy. (*He exits.*)

Blackout on **Leah**.

Scene Three

Lyman *is softly snoring; a deep troubled sleep, however; bad dreams, muttering, an arm raised in a gesture.*

Tom *enters with* **Nurse**. *She raises* **Lyman**'s *eyelid.*

Nurse   He still goes in and out but you can try him.

Tom   Lyman? Can you hear me? (**Lyman** *stops snoring but eyes remain shut.*) It's Tom Wilson.

Nurse   Keep going, he shouldn't be staying under this much by now.

Tom   Lyman, it's Tom.

Lyman (*opens his eyes*)   *You* in the store?

Tom   It's the hospital.

Lyman   Hospital? Oh right, right . . . Jesus, I was dreaming of my father's store; every time he looked at me he'd shake his head and say, 'Hopeless case.' (*Laughs tiredly, trying to focus*.) Give me a second; little mixed up. How'd you get here?

Tom   Theodora called me.

Lyman   Theodora?

Tom   Your car is registered in the city so the state police called her.

Lyman   I had some weird dream that she and Bessie . . . (*Breaks off.*) They're not here, are they?

Nurse   I told you your wife came . . .

Tom (*to* **Nurse**)   Excuse us, please?

Nurse   But I told him. (*She exits.*)

Tom   They've met, Lyman.

Lyman (*pause; he struggles to orient himself*)   Theo . . . didn't collapse, did she?

Tom   Yes, but she's come around, she'll be all right.

Lyman   I don't understand it, I think I dreamed the whole thing . . .

Tom   Well, that wouldn't be too difficult, it's all pretty inevitable.

Lyman   Why're you being so brutal?

Tom   There's no time to fool around, you've got things to decide. It's all over television . . .

Lyman   Oh.—Have you met her?—Leah? I'm finished.

Tom   We've had a talk. She's a considerable woman.

Lyman (*gratefully*)   Isn't she?—She's furious, too, huh?

Tom   Well, what do you expect?

Lyman   See . . . I thought I'd somehow divorce Theo later.—But it sort of settled in where I had both of them. And after a while it didn't seem so godawful . . . What about Bessie?

Tom   It's hit her pretty bad, I guess.

Lyman   God, and poor little Benny! Jesus, if I could go through the ceiling and just disappear.

Tom   The television is flogging it. I think you ought to issue a press statement to cut the whole thing short. As to your intentions.

Lyman   What intentions? Just give each of them whatever they want. I'll probably go and live somewhere . . . maybe like Brazil or something . . .

Tom   You won't try to hold on to either of them.

Lyman   Are you mad? They wouldn't have anything to do with me. My God . . . (*He turns away, tears in his eyes.*) How could I have destroyed everything like this!—my character! (*Higher intensity:*) Why did I drive into that storm?—I can't understand it! I had the room in the Howard Johnson's, I think I was even in bed . . . figured I'd wait out the storm there . . . Why'd I go out into it again?

Tom   Can you give Theo a few minutes? She wants to say goodbye.

Lyman   How can I face her? Ask her to wait till tomorrow, maybe I'll feel a little better and . . .

Theo *and* **Bessie** *enter;* **Lyman** *does not see them, as they are above him.*

Tom   They're here, Lyman.

Lyman *closes his eyes, breathing fast.* **Bessie**, *holding* **Theo** *by the elbow, accompanies her to the bedside.*

Bessie (*whispering with some shock*)   Look at his bandages! (*Turning away.*) Oh, Mother!

Theo   Stop that. (*Bending to* **Lyman***:*) Lyman? (*He can't get himself to speak.*) It's Theodora.

Lyman (*opening his eyes*)   Hi.

Theo   How are you feeling?

Lyman   Not too bad now. I hope I make sense with all this painkiller . . . Is that you, Bessie?

Bessie   I'm only here because of Mother.

Lyman   Oh. Okay. I'm sorry, Bess—I mean that my character's so bad. But I'm proud that you have enough strength to despise me.

Bessie   But who wouldn't?

Lyman   Good! (*His voice starts to break but he controls himself.*) That was well-spoken, sweetie.

Bessie (*with quick anger*)   Don't call me that . . .

Theo (*to* **Bessie**)   Shhh! (*She has been observing him in silence.*) Lyman?—Is it true?

Lyman *closes his eyes.*

I have to hear it from you. Did you marry that woman?

Deep snores.

(*More urgently:*) Lyman?

Bessie (*points*)   He's not really sleeping!

Theo   Did you have a child with that woman? Lyman? I insist!!! I insist!!!

Lyman *emerges from the upstage side of the bed, hands clapped to his ears, while* **Theo** *and* **Bessie** *continue addressing the bed, as though he were still in it.*

Light change: an ethereal colorlessness now, air devoid of pigment.

Lyman (*agonized cry, ears still covered*)   I hear you!

Theo *continues to address the bed, and* **Bessie** *is fixed on it as well, but their attitude becomes formalized as they become part of his vision.*

Theo   What in God's name have you done!

Almost writhing in conflict, **Lyman** *clears his throat. He remains a distance upstage of the bed.*

Bessie (*bent over the bed*)   Shh! He's saying something!

Lyman   I realize . . . how crazy it sounds, Theodora . . . (*Breaks off.*)

Theo   Yes?

Lyman   . . . I'm not really sure, but . . . I wonder if this crash . . . was maybe to sort of subconsciously . . . get you both to . . . meet one another, finally.

Theo (*with disgust*)   Meet *her?*

Lyman   I know it sounds absurd but . . .

Theo   Absurd! —It's disgusting! She's exactly the type who forgets to wash out her panties.

Lyman (*wincing, but with a certain pleasurable recognition*)   I *knew* you'd say that! —I admit it, though, there is a sloppy side to her . . .

Theo   She's the worst generation in our history—screw anybody in pants, then drop their litters like cats, and spout mystic credos on cosmic responsibility, ecology, and human rights!

Lyman   To my dying day I will stand amazed at your ability to speak in complete paragraphs!

Theo   I insist you explain this to me yourself. Lyman? Lyman!

Leah *enters.* **Theo** *reacts instantly.*

There'll be no one in here but family! (*To* **Bessie**.) Get the nurse!

Leah (*despite* **Theo**, *approaches the cast, but with uncertainty about his reaction to her*)   Lyman?

Theo (*to* **Tom**)   Get her out of here! (**Tom** *is immobile, and she goes to him furiously.*) She does not belong here!

Leah (*to the cast, with a certain warmth*)   It's me, Lyme. Can you hear me?

Theo (*rushing threateningly toward* **Leah**)   Get out, get out, get out . . . !

Just as she is about to lay hands on **Leah**, **Lyman** *throws his arms up and cries imploringly.*

Lyman   I want everybody to lie down!

The three women instantly de-animate as though suddenly falling under the urgency of his control. **Lyman** *gestures, without actually touching them, and causes* **Theo** *and* **Leah** *to lie on the bed.*

Leah (*as she lies down; voice soft, remote*)   What am I going to tell Benny? Oh gee whiz, Lyman, why did you . . . ?

Theo (*lying down beside* **Leah**)   You have a bitter smell, you should use something.

Leah   I have, but he likes it.

Theo   Blah. (*To* **Lyman**:) And what would you say if one of us took another man to bed and asked you to lie next to him?

Lyman (*lifting off her glasses*)   Oh, I'd kill him, dear; but you're a lady, Theodora; the delicate sculpture of your noble eye, your girlish faith in me and your disillusion; your idealism and your unadmitted greed for wealth; the awkward tenderness of your wooden fingers, your incurably Protestant cooking; your savoir-faire and your sexual inexperience; your sensible shoes and devoted motherhood, your intolerant former radicalism and stalwart love of country now—your Theodorism! Who can ever take your place!

Leah (*laughing*)   Why am I laughing!!

Lyman   Because you're an anarchist, my darling! (*He stretches out on both of them.*) Oh, what pleasure, what intensity! Your countercurrents are like bare live wires! (*Kisses each in turn.*) I'd have no problem defending both of you to the death! Oh the double heat of two blessed wives—this is heaven! (*Rests his head on* **Leah** *while holding* **Theo**'s *hand to his cheek.*)

Leah   Listen, you've got to make up your mind about something.

Lyman   I'm only delaying as long as possible, let's delay it till we all die! Delay, delay, how delicious, my loving Leah, is delay!

Theo (*sits up*)   How you can still go on talking about love is beyond my understanding.

Lyman   And still I love you, Theodora, although certain parts of your body fill me with *rage!*

Theo   So you simply got yourself some other parts instead.

Leah, *still lying on her back, raises one leg in the air, and her skirt slides down, exposing her thigh.*

Lyman (*replying to* **Theo**, *kissing* **Leah***'s thigh*)   That's the truth, yes—at least it was all flesh at first.

Leah (*stretching out her arms and her body*)   Oh, how good that was! I'm still pulsing to the tips of my toes. (**Theo** *helps him into shirt and trousers and hands him a jacket.*)

You're really healthy, aren't you.

Lyman (*they are moving out of* **Theo***'s area*)   You mean for my age? Yes.

Leah   I did not mean that!

Loud knocking heard. She turns upstage with slight shock. A man's angry voice, muffled words. She stands motionless.

Lyman   You okay?

Leah   It's nothing! Do you have time for a walk?

Lyman   My health is terrific; in fact, it keeps threatening my dignity.

A park bench appears.

Leah   Why!

Lyman   Well, how do I come to be lounging in a park with a girl, and on a working day! I really hadn't planned to do that this afternoon. Did you know I was going to?

Leah   No . . . but I never do.

Lyman   Really? But you seem so organized.

Leah   In business; but not in pleasure.

Lyman   What surprised me was the openness of your laughter with those heavy executives at the table.

Leah   Well, your presentation was so funny, I'd heard you were a real brain, not a comic.

Lyman   Well, insurance is basically comical, isn't it?—at least pathetic.

Leah   Why?

Lyman   You're buying immortality, aren't you?—reaching out of your grave to pay the bills and remind people of your life? It's poetry. The soul was once immortal, now we've got an insurance policy.

Leah   You sound pretty cynical about it.

Lyman   Not at all—I started as a writer, nobody lusts after the immortal like a writer.

Leah   How'd you get into insurance?

Lyman   Pure accident. How'd you?

Leah   My mother had died, my dad had his stroke, and insurance was something I could do from home. Dad knew a lot of people, being a doctor, so the thing just took off.

Lyman   Don't take this wrong—but you know what I find terrifically sexy about you?

Leah   What?

Lyman   Your financial independence. Horrible, huh?

Leah   Why?—(*wryly*)—Whatever helps, helps.

Lyman   You don't sound married, are you?

Leah   It's a hell of a time to ask! (*They laugh, come closer.*) I can't see myself getting married . . . not yet anyway. —Incidentally, have you been listening to me?

Lyman   Yes, but my attention keeps wandering toward a warm and furry place . . . (*She laughs, delighted.*) It's funny, my generation got married to show its maturity, yours stays single for the same reason.

Leah   That's good!

Lyman   How happy I am! (*Sniffs his hands.*) Sitting in Elmira in the sun with you, and your scent still on my hands! God!—all the different ways there are to try to be real! —I don't know the connection, but when I turned twenty I sold three poems to *The New Yorker* and a story to *Harper's*, and the first thing I bought was a successful blue suit to impress my father how real I was even though a writer. He ran an appetizer store on Fortieth Street and Ninth Avenue. (*Grinning, near laughter.*) And he sees the suit and says, 'How much you pay?' And I said, 'Twenty-nine-fifty,' thinking I'd got a terrific bargain. And he says, 'Pray God keep an eye on you the rest of your life.'

Leah (*laughs*)   That's awful!

Lyman   No!—it spurred me on! (*Laughs.*) He had two pieces of wisdom—never trust anybody, and never forgive. Funny, it's like magic, I simply can't trace how we got into bed.

Leah (*a glance at her watch*)   I really have to get back to the office.—But is Lyman an Albanian name?

Lyman   Lyman's the judge's name in Worcester, Massachusetts, who gave my father his citizenship. Felt is short for Feltman, my mother's name, because my father's was unpronounceable and they wanted a successful American for a son.

Leah   Then your mother was Jewish.

Lyman   And the source of all my conflicts. In the Jewish heart is a lawyer and a judge, in the Albanian a bandit defying the government with a knife.

Leah   What a surprise you are! (*She stands, and he does.*)

Lyman   Being so silly?

Leah   Being so interesting, and in the insurance business.

Lyman (*taking her hand*)   When was the moment?—I'm just curious.

Leah   I don't know . . . I guess at the conference table I suddenly thought, 'He's basically talking to me.' But then I figured, this is probably why he's such a great salesman, because everybody he talks to feels loved.

Lyman   You know?—I've never before with a Jewish girl.

Leah   Well, you're my first Albanian.

Lyman   There's something venerable in your eyes. Not old—ancient. Like our peoples.

Leah (*touching his cheek*)   Take care, dear.

Lyman (*as she passes before him to leave, he takes her hand*)   Why do I feel I know nothing about you?

Leah (*shrugs, smiles*)   Maybe you weren't listening . . . which I don't mind if it's in a good cause.

Lyman (*letting go of her hand*)   I walk in the valley of your thighs. (*She laughs, gives him a quick kiss.*) When you move away now, would you turn back to me for a moment?

Leah (*amused*)   Sure, why?

Lyman (*half-kidding in his romanticism*)   I have to take a small commuter plane and if I die I want that vision as I go down—

Leah (*backing away with a wave*)   'Bye, Lyman . . .

Lyman   Can I ask who that fellow was banging on your apartment door?

Leah (*caught off-guard*)   Somebody I used to go with . . . he was angry, that's all.

Lyman   Are you afraid of him?

Leah (*shrugs in an accepted uncertainty*)   See you, dear.

She turns and walks a few yards, then halts and turns her head to look back at him over her shoulder. She exits.

Lyman   Beautiful. (*Alone:*) Miraculous. (*Thinks for a moment.*) Still . . . was it really all *that* great? (*Takes out a cell phone, troubled.*) Theo?—hi, darling, I'm just about to take off. Oh, definitely, it has the makings of a much bigger operation; had a talk

with Aetna's chief rep up here, and she's agreed to take us on, so
I'll probably be spending more time here. —Yes, a woman; she's
got a great agency, I might try to buy into her. —Listen, dear, how
about you flying up here and we rent a car and drive through
Cherry Valley—it's bursting into bloom now! —Oh, I forgot;
no-no, you'd better go to your meeting then; it's okay; no, it just
suddenly hit me how quickly it's all going by and . . . You ever
have the feeling that you never *really* got to know anybody?

She never has; he resents it, and a sharpness enters his voice.

Well, yes, I do feel that sometimes, very much; sometimes I feel
I'm going to vanish without a trace, Theo! (*Unhappily now, with
hidden anger, the romance gone.*) Theo, dear, it's nothing against
you, I only meant that with all the analysis and the novels and the
Freuds we're still as opaque and unknowable as some line of
statues in a church wall. (*He hangs up. Now a light strikes the cast
on the bed. He moves to it and looks down at himself.* **Bessie**,
Theo, *and* **Leah** *are standing motionless around the bed and* **Tom**
is off to the one side, observing. **Lyman** *slowly lifts his arms and
raises his face like a suppliant.*) We're all in a cave . . . (*The three
women now begin to move, ever so slightly at first; their heads are
turning as they appear to be searching for the sight of something
far away or overhead or on the floor.*) . . . where we entered to
make love or money or fame. It's dark in here, as dark as sleep,
and each one moves blindly, searching for another, to touch,
hoping to touch and afraid; and hoping, and afraid.

As he speaks, the women and **Tom** *move in a criss-crossing path,
just missing one another, spreading farther and farther across the
stage until one by one they disappear.* **Lyman** *has moved above the
bed where his cast lies.*

So now . . . now that we're here . . . what are we going to say?

Blackout.

Act Two

Scene One

The hospital waiting room. **Tom** *is seated with* **Theo**.

Tom Really, Theo, I wish you'd let Bessie take you back to the city.

Theo Please stop repeating that! (*Slight pause.*) I need to talk to him . . . I'll never see him again. I can't simply walk away. Is my head trembling?

Tom A little, maybe. Should you let one of the doctors look at you?

Theo I'll be all right, my family has a tendency to tremors, I've had it for years when I'm tense. What time is it?

Tom Give them a few minutes more. —You seem pale.

Theo (*pressing fingers against her temples to steady herself*) When you spoke with this woman . . . was there any feeling about . . . what she has in mind?

Tom She's as much in shock as you. The child was her main concern.

Theo Really? I wouldn't have thought so.

Tom Oh, I think he means everything to her.

Theo (*begrudgingly*) Well, that's nice. Messes like this are basically comical, aren't they—until you come to the children. I'm very worried about Bessie. She lies there staring at the ceiling. She can hardly talk without starting to weep. He's been her . . . her world. (*She begins to fill up.*) You're right, I think I'll go. It just seemed unfinished, somehow . . . but maybe it's better to leave it this way . . . (*Starts for her bag, stops.*) I don't know what to do. One minute I could kill him, the next I wonder if some . . . aberration got into him . . .

Leah *enters. They did not expect to see each other. A momentary pause.* **Leah** *sits.*

Leah   Good afternoon.

Tom   Good afternoon.

Awkward silence.

Leah (*asking*)   He's not in his room?

Theo (*as it is difficult for her to address* **Leah***, she turns to her slowly*)   They're treating his eye.

Leah   His eye?

Tom   It's nothing serious, he tried to climb out his window. Probably in his sleep. His eyelid was slightly scratched by a rhododendron.

Theo (*making a stab at communication*)   He must not have realized he's on the ground floor.

Short pause.

Leah   Hm! That's interesting, because a friend of ours, Ted Colby, called last night—he's a commander of the state police here. They'd put up a wooden barrier across the Mount Morgan road when it got so icy; and he thinks Lyman moved the barrier aside.

Tom   How could they know it was him?

Leah   There was only one set of tire tracks.

Theo   Oh my God.

Leah   He's worried about him. They're good friends, they go hunting together.

Theo   Lyman hunts?

Leah   Oh sure. (**Theo** *shakes her head incredulously.*) But I can't imagine him in that kind of depression, can you?

Tom   Actually . . . yes, I think I can.

Leah   Really. He's always seemed so . . . up with me, and happy. (**Theo** *glances from her, irked, then away.* **Leah** *glances at her* *watch.*) I just have to settle some business with him for a few minutes, I won't be in your way.

Theo   *My* way? You're free to do anything you like, as far as I'm concerned.

Leah (*slightly taken aback*)   Yes . . . the same with me . . . in your case. (*Beat.*) I mean as far as I'm concerned. (*The hostility turns her to look at her watch again.*) I want to tell you . . . I almost feel worse for you, somehow, than for myself.

Theo (*gives a hard laugh*)   Why! Do I seem *that* old? (*The second rebuff stiffens* **Leah**.) I shouldn't have said that. I apologize. I'm exhausted.

Leah (*letting it pass*)   How is your daughter?—she still here?

Theo (*a hostile color despite everything*)   In the motel. She's devastated.

Tom   Your boy taking it all right?

Leah   No, it's wracked him, it's terrible. (*To* **Theo***:*) I thought Lyman might have some idea how to deal with him, the kid's always idolized him so. I'm really at my wits' end.

Theo (*bitterly angry, but contained*)   We are his dust; we billow up behind his steps and settle again when he passes by. Billie Holiday . . . (*She touches her forehead.*) I can't recall when she died, it's quite a while, isn't it.

Tom   Billie Holiday? Why?

Tom *and* **Leah** *observe, puzzled, as* **Theo** *stares in silence. Then . . .*

Leah   Why don't I come back in a couple of hours—I've got a two o'clock conference call and it's getting a bit late . . . (*She stands, goes to* **Theo***, and, extending her hand.*) Well, if we don't meet again . . .

Theo (*touching her hand briefly, hostility momentarily overcome*)   . . . Do you understand this?

Leah   It's baffling. He's raced the Mount Morgan road, he knows what it's like, even in summer.

Theo   Raced? You mean cars?

Leah   Sure. He has a Lotus and a Z. He had a Ferrari, but he totaled it. (**Theo** *turns and stares into space, stunned.*) I was thinking before . . .

Theo   He's always been terrified of speed; he never drives over sixty . . .

Leah   . . . He reminds me of a frog . . .

Theo   A frog?

Leah   . . . I mean you never know when you look at a frog whether it's the same one you just saw or a different one. (*To* **Tom***:*) When you talk to him—the television is hounding us; he really has to make a definite statement to stop all this stupid speculation.

Theo   What speculation?

Leah   You've seen the *Daily News,* haven't you?

Theo   What!

Leah   We're both on the front page with a headline . . .

Tom (*to* **Theo***, placating*)   It's unimportant . . .

Theo (*to* **Leah***)   What's the headline?

Leah   'Who gets Lyman?'

Theo   How dare they!

Tom   Don't be upset. (*To* **Leah***:*) I'll get a statement from him this afternoon . . .

Leah   Goodbye, Mrs. . . . . (*Stops herself; a short laugh.*) I was going to call you Mrs. Felt, but . . . (*Correcting again. . . .*) Well you are, aren't you—I guess I'm the one who's not! I'll come by about three or so. (**Leah** *exits.*)

Theo   She wants him back, doesn't she.

Tom   Why?

Theo (*gives her little laugh*)   Didn't you hear it?—she's the one he was happy with!

Tom   Oh, I don't think she meant . . .

Theo (*her fierce competitiveness aroused*)   That's *all* she meant. —I pity her, though, with such a young child. (*She fumes in silence.*) *Can* it have been suicide?

Tom   Frankly, I'd almost hope so, in a way.

Theo   You mean it would indicate a moral conscience?

Tom   Yes. —But I'm wondering . . . maybe he just wanted to change his life; become a completely different person . . .

Theo (*stares for a moment*)   . . . Maybe not so different.

Tom   How do you mean?

Theo (*a long hesitation*)   I don't know why I'm still trying to protect him—he tried to kill me once.

Tom   You're not serious.

Lyman *appears in sunlight in swim trunks, inhaling deeply on a boat deck. She begins walking toward him.*

Theo   Oh yes! I didn't know this woman existed then, but I see now it was just about the time they had either married or were on the verge. (*As she moves toward* **Lyman***, her coat slides off, revealing her in a swimsuit.*) He seemed very strange, unreal. We'd gone for a two-day sail off Montauk . . .

Lyman *is doing breathing exercises.*

Lyman   The morning mist rising from the sea is always like the first day of the world . . . the 'oysterygods and the visigods . . .'

Theo *enters into* **Lyman**'*s acting area.*

Theo   *Finnegans Wake.*

Lyman   I'll get the weather. (*Kneels, tunes a radio; static.*) Is that a new suit? It's sexy as hell.

Theo   Two years ago. You bought it for me in San Diego.

Lyman (*mimes a pistol to his head*)   Bang.

Announcer (*voice-over:*)   . . . Due to the unusually warm spring tides there've been several shark sightings off Montauk . . . one is reported to be twelve to fourteen feet long . . . (*Heavy static intervenes;* **Lyman** *mimes switching the radio off.*)

Lyman   Jesus.

Theo   Oh that's ridiculous, it's only May! I'm going in for a dip . . . (*She looks out over the ocean.*)

Lyman   But the radio man said . . .

Theo   Nonsense. I've sailed around here since my childhood, and so did my grandparents—there are never sharks until July if at all, the water's much too cold. Come in with me?

Lyman   I'm the Mediterranean type—we're unreliable and hate cold water. I know I shouldn't say this, Theo, but how you can hang on to your convictions in the face of a report like that . . . just seems . . . I don't know—fanatical.

Theo (*with a hard, determined laugh*)   Now that is really uncalled for! You're just as stubborn as I am when you're committed to something.

Lyman   Goddammit, you're right! And I love your convictions!—go ahead, I'll keep an eye out.

Theo (*with loving laughter*)   You simply can't stand me contradicting you, darling, but it's the best exercise for your character.

Lyman   Right! And a miserable character it is. Into the ocean! (*He leaves her side, scans the ocean.*)

Theo (*bends for a dive*)   On the mark . . . get set . . .

Lyman (*pointing left*)   What's that out there!

Theo   No, sharks always move, that's a log.

Lyman   Oh right. Okay, jump in.

Theo   I'll run in! Wait, let me warm up. (*Backs up to make a run for it.*) Join me! Come on.

Lyman   I can't, dear, I fear death.

She is behind him, running in place. His back is to her and his eye catches sight of something toward the right front; his mouth opens, eyes staring in horror following the moving shark. She bends to start her run.

Theo   Okay, one . . . and a two . . . and a . . . three! (*She runs and as she comes abreast of him he suddenly, at the last moment, reaches out and stops her at the edge.*)

Lyman   Stop!

He points front; she looks, horror rising on her face as their eyes follow the fish.

Theo   My God, the *size* of him! Ahhh . . . ! (*She bursts into tears of released terror; he takes her into his arms.*)

Lyman   Honey, when are you going to trust something I say!

Theo   Oh, I'm going to be sick . . . !

About to vomit, she bends and rushes into darkness. Lights go out on **Lyman** *and up on* **Tom** *in the waiting room; he is staring straight ahead, listening. The light widens and finds* **Theo** *standing in her fur coat.*

Tom   That sounds like he saved you.

Theo   Yes, I've always tried to think of it that way, too, but I have to face everything, now—(*coming downstage; newly distressed by the memory*)—it was not quite at the top of his voice. I mean, it wasn't . . .

Light flares up on **Lyman** *in his trunks. At top voice and in horror he shouts . . .*

Lyman   Stop! (*He stands mesmerized looking at the shark below. Blackout on* **Lyman**.)

Theo   It was more like . . .

Lights flare up again on **Lyman**, *and he merely semi-urgently—as he did in the scene—shouts . . .*

Lyman   Stop.

Blackout on **Lyman**.

Theo   I tell you he was on the verge of letting me go.

Tom   Come on, Theo, you can't really believe that. I mean, how could you have gone on living with him?

Theo   How I've gone on? (*A bitter and embarrassed smile.*) Well, we did have two serious breakups and . . . months have gone by without . . . relations. (*Gradually becomes furious.*) No, damnit, I'm not going to evade this anymore. —Maybe I've gone on because I'm corrupt, Tom. I certainly wasn't once, but who knows, now? He's rich, isn't he? And vastly respected, and what would I do with myself alone? Why does anybody stay together, once they realize who they're with? (*Suddenly livid.*) What the hell am I hanging around here for? This is the stupidest thing I've ever done in my life! (*Indignantly grabs her bag.*)

Tom   You love him, Theo. (*Physically stops her.*) Please go home, will you? And give it a few weeks before you decide anything? (*She stifles a sob as he embraces her.*) I know how crazy this sounds, but part of him worships you. I'm sure of it.

Theo (*suddenly screams in his face*)   I hate him! I hate him! (*She is rigid, pale, and he grips her shoulders to steady her. A pause.*) I must lie down. We'll probably go back to the city tonight. But call me if he wakes up. —It's so hard to just walk away without knowing what happened. —Or maybe I should just leave . . . (*She passes her hand across her brow.*) Do I look strange?

Tom   Just tired. Come, I'll find you a cab.

Theo   It's only a few blocks, I need the air. (*Starting off, turns back.*) Amazing how beautiful the country still is up here. Like nothing bad had ever happened in the world. (*She exits.*)

Alone, **Tom** *stands staring into space, arms folded, trying to figure out an approach.*

Blackout.

Scene Two

Lyman's *room. He is deeply asleep, snoring placidly at first. Now he starts muttering.*

Nurse   Whyn't you take some time off? You do more work asleep than most of us awake. You ought to come up ice fishing with us sometime, that'll slow you down.

Nurse *goes out. Now there is a tensing up, he is groaning in his sleep.* **Leah** *and* **Theo** *appear on either side of him, but on elevated platforms, like two stone deities; they are in kitchen aprons, wifely ribbons tying up their hair. But there is something menacing about their deathly stillness as the sepulchral dream-light finds them, motionless in this tableau. After a long moment they reanimate. As in life they are reserved, each measuring herself against the other. Their manner of speaking is godlike, deathly.*

Theo   I wouldn't mind it at all if you did some of the cooking, I'm not all that super.

Leah (*generously*)   I hear you make good desserts, though.

Theo   Apple cobbler, yes; gingerbread with whipped cream. (*Gaining confidence.*) And exceptional waffles for breakfast, with real maple syrup, although he's had to cut out the sausages.

Leah   I can do potato pancakes and segadina goulash.

Theo (*disapproving*)   And all that paprika?

Leah   It has to be blended in, of course.

Theo (*at a loss, sensing defeat*)   Ah, blended in! I'm afraid I couldn't do something like that.

Leah (*smiling, brutally pressing her advantage*)   Oh yes, blended in and really blended *in!* And my gefilte fish is feather-light. (*Clapping her cupped palms together.*) I wet my hands and keep patting it till it shapes up just perfect!

Theo (*struggling, at a loss*)   He does love my glazed ham. Yes!—and my boiled tongue. (*A sudden bright idea.*) Custard!

Leah (*generously*)   You can do all the custard and glazed ham and I'll do all the gefilte fish and goulash . . . *and* the blending in.

Theo   But may I do *some?* Once or twice a month, perhaps?

Leah   Let's leave it up to him—some months you can do more . . .

Theo   Yes!—and some months you.

Leah   'Kay! Would you wash out my panties?

Theo   Certainly. As long as he tells me my lies.

Leah   Good! Then you'll have your lies and I'll have mine!

Theo and **Leah**   Hurrah for the menu!

Leah (*filled with admiration*)   You certainly have class!

Lyman *chuckles in his sleep as they emerge from their matronly costumes, now dressed in sexy black tight-fitting body stockings and high heels and, slithering toward each other, kiss, turn toward the bed and as he laughs suddenly raise long daggers and chop at him again and again. He is shouting and writhing as* **Nurse** *rushes in and the women disappear.*

Nurse   All right now, let's come back, dear, come on back . . .

He stops struggling and opens his eyes.

Lyman   Wah. Oh. What dreams. God, how I'd like to be dead.

Nurse   Don't start feeling sorry for yourself; you know what they say—come down off the cross, they need the wood.

Lyman   I'm suffocating, can't you open a window?

Nurse   Not anymore, I can't.

Lyman   Huh? Oh listen, that's ridiculous, I wasn't really trying to climb out . . .

Nurse   Well, you did a pretty good imitation. Your lawyer's asking can he come in . . .

Lyman   I thought he'd gone back to New York. I look terrible?

Nurse (*swabbing his face and hands*)   You takin' it too hard. Be different if you deserted those women, but anybody can see how well taken care of they are. . . .

Lyman   Go on, you don't kid me, Logan—underneath all this cool you know you're as shocked as hell.

Nurse   Go on, brush your teeth. (*As he does.*) The last shock I had come off a short in my vacuum cleaner . . . (*he laughs, then groans in pain.*) One thing I *have* been wondering, though.

Lyman   What've you been wondering?

Nurse   Whatever got into you to actually marry that woman?— man as smart as you?

Lyman   Were you talking about ice before?

Nurse   Ice? Oh, you mean . . . ya, we go ice fishing on the lake, me, my husband, and my boy—you're remembering a lot better now.

Lyman (*staring*)   Not being married is going to feel very strange—like suddenly your case has been dismissed and you don't have to be in court anymore.

Nurse   Don't you talk bad about those women; they don't look mean to me.

Lyman   Why I married her? —I'm very attracted to women who smell like fruit; Leah smelled like a pink, ripe cantaloupe. And when she smiled, her clothes seemed to drop off. I'd never been so jealous. I swear, if a hundred women walked past me on a sidewalk I could pick out the clack of Leah's heels. I even loved lying in bed listening to the quiet splash of her bathwater. And of course slipping into her pink cathedral . . .

Nurse   You have the dirtiest mind I ever seen on an educated man.

Lyman   I couldn't lose her, Logan, and that's the best reason to marry anybody, unless you're married already.

Nurse   I'll get your lawyer, okay? (*He seems suddenly overcome; weeps.*) Now don't you start that cryin' again . . .

Lyman   It's just my children . . . you can't imagine how they respected me . . . (*Bracing himself.*) But nobody's any better, goddammit!

Tom *enters.*

Tom   May I come in?

Lyman (*uncertainly, trying to read* **Tom**)   Hi! I thought you'd gone back—something happen?

Tom   Can we talk?

Nurse *exits.*

Lyman   If you can bear it. (*Grins.*) You despise me, Tom?

Tom   I'm still staggering. I don't know what to think.

Lyman   Sure you do, but that's okay. (*His charming grin.*) So, what's up?

Tom   I've been discussing things with the women . . .

Lyman   I thought I told you—or did I?—just give them what they want. Within reason, I mean.

Tom   I really believe Theo'd like to find a way to forgive you.

Lyman   Impossible!

Tom   She's a great spirit, Lyman.

Lyman   . . . Not that great; I'd have to live on my knees for the rest of my life.

Tom   Maybe not—if you were clear about yourselves . . .

Lyman   I'm pretty clear now—I'm a selfish son of a bitch. But I have loved the truth.

Tom   And what's the truth?

Lyman   A man can be faithful to himself or to other people—but not to both. At least not happily. We all know this, but it's immoral to admit that the first law of life is betrayal; why else did those rabbis pick Cain and Abel to open the Bible? Cain felt betrayed by God, so he betrayed Him and killed his brother.

Tom   But the Bible doesn't end there, does it.

Lyman   Jesus Christ? I can't worship self-denial; it's just not true for me. We're all ego, kid, ego plus an occasional heart-felt prayer.

Tom   Then why'd you bother building one of the most socially responsible companies in America?

Lyman   The truth? I did that twenty-five years ago, when I was a righteous young man; but I am an unrighteous middle-aged man now, so all I have left is to try not to live with too many lies. (*Suddenly collapsing within.*) —Why must I see them? . . . What can I say to them? Christ, if I could only lose consciousness! (*Rocking side to side in anguish.*) . . . Advise me, Tom, tell me something.

Tom   Maybe you ought to give up trying to seem so strong.

Slight pause.

Lyman   What do you want me to say, I'm a loser?

Tom   Well, right now, aren't you?

Lyman   No, goddammit! A loser has lived somebody else's life, I've lived my own; crappy as it may seem, it's mine.—And I'm no worse than anybody else!—Now answer that, and don't kid me.

Tom   All right, I won't kid you; I think you've done these women terrible harm.

Lyman   You do.

Tom   If you want to get off this dime you're on I'd begin by confronting the damage I'd done—I think you've raked Theo's soul.

Lyman   I've also given her an interesting life, a terrific daughter, and made her very rich. I mean, exactly what harm are you talking about?

Tom   Lyman, you deceived her . . .

Lyman (*fury overtaking him*)   But she couldn't have had all that if I hadn't deceived her!—you know as well as I that nobody could live with Theo for more than a month without some relief! I've suffered at least as much as she has in this marriage!

Tom (*demurring*)   Well . . .

Lyman   . . . Now listen, you want the rock-bottom truth?—I curse the day I ever laid eyes on her and I don't *want* her forgiveness!

Tom   For Pete's sake, don't get angry . . .

Lyman   I ever tell you how we met?—let's stop pretending this marriage was made in heaven, for Christ's sake!—I was hitchhiking back from Cornell; nineteen innocent years of age; I'm standing beside the road with my suitcase and I go behind a bush. This minister sees the suitcase and stops, gives me a ride, and I end up at an Audubon Society picnic, where lo and behold, I meet his daughter, Theodora.—Had I taken that suitcase with me behind the bush I'd never have met her!—And serious people are still talking about the moral purpose of the universe!

Tom   Give or take a bad patch or two, you've had the best marriage of anyone I've ever met.

Lyman (*with a sigh*)   I know.—Look, we're all the same; a man is a fourteen-room house—in the bedroom he's asleep with his intelligent wife, in his living room he's rolling around with some bare-assed girl, in the library he's paying his taxes, in the yard he's raising tomatoes, and in the cellar he's making a bomb to blow it all up. And nobody's different . . . Except you, maybe. Are you?

Tom   I don't raise tomatoes . . . Listen, the TV is flogging the story and it's humiliating for the women; let's settle on a statement and be done with it. What do you want?

Lyman   What I always wanted: both of them.

Tom   Be serious . . .

Lyman   I know these women and they still love me! It's only what they think they're *supposed* to feel that's confusing them.— Do I sound crazy?

Tom   Listen, I forgot to tell you—Jeff Huddleston called me this morning; heard it on the radio; he insists you resign from the board.

Lyman   Not on your life! That fat fraud—Jeff Huddleston's got a woman stashed in Trump Tower and two in L.A.

Tom   *Huddleston!*

Lyman   He offered to loan me one once! Huddleston has more outside ass than a Nevada whorehouse!

Tom   But he doesn't marry them.

Lyman   Right!—in other words, what I really violated was the law of hypocrisy.

Tom   Unfortunately that's the one that operates.

Lyman   Not with me, baby! I may be a bastard but I am not a hypocrite! I am not quitting my company! What's Leah saying . . . anything?

Tom   She's stunned. But frankly, I'm not sure she's out of the question either . . . if that's the move you wanted to make.

Lyman (*deeply touched*)   What size these women have! (*Weeping threatens again.*) Oh Tom, I'm lost!

Bessie *and* **Theo** *enter.* **Theo** *stands beside his bed staring at him without expression.* **Bessie** *doesn't so much as look at him. After a long moment . . .*

(*Downing fear*) My God, Theo—thank you . . . I mean for coming. I didn't expect you . . .

She sits down in a potent silence. **Bessie** *stands, fiercely aloof. He is openly and awkwardly ashamed.*

Hi, Bessie.

Bessie   I'm here for her sake, she wanted to say something to you. (*Hurrying her along.*) Mother?

But **Theo** *takes no notice, staring at* **Lyman** *with a fixed, unreadable smile. After a long, awkward moment . . .*

Lyman (*to fill the void*)   How are you feeling today? I hear you were . . .

Theo (*dead flat, cutting him off*)   I won't be seeing you again, Lyman.

Lyman (*despite everything, a bit of a blow—slight pause*)   Yes. Well . . . I guess there's no use in apologizing. . . . But I am sorry, Theo.

Theo   I can't leave my life lying all over the floor like this.

Lyman   I'll talk about anything you like.

Theo   I seem confused but I'm not; there's just so much that I . . . that I don't want bottled up in me anymore.

Lyman   Sure, I understand.

Theo   —Do you remember that young English instructor whose wife walked out on him—his advice to you about sex?

Lyman   An English instructor? At Cornell, you mean?

Theo   'Bend it in half,' he said, 'and tie a rubber band around it.'

Lyman (*laughing, a little alarmed*)   Oh sure, Jim Donaldson!

Theo   Everyone used to laugh at that.

Lyman (*her smile is empty, his charm desperate*)   Right! 'Bend it in half and . . .' (*Continues a strained chuckling.*)

Theo (*cutting him off*)   I *hated* you laughing at that; it showed a vulgar and disgusting side of you. I was ashamed . . . for you and for myself.

Lyman (*brought up short*)   I see. But that's so long ago, Theo . . .

Theo   I want to tell you that I nearly ended it right then and there, but I thought I was too inexperienced to make a judgment. But I was right—you *were* a vulgar, unfeeling man, and you are still.

Anxiously, **Lyman** *glances over to* **Bessie** *for help or explanation of this weirdness.*

Lyman   I see. Well, I guess our whole life was a mistake then. (*Angered but attempting charm.*) But I made a good living.

Bessie   Please, Mother, let's go, he's mocking you, can't you hear it?

Lyman (*flaring up*)   Must I not defend myself? Please go ahead, Theo, I understand what you're saying, and it's okay, it's what you feel.

Theo (*seemingly relaxed*)   —What was the name of the river, about half an hour's walk past the Chemistry building?

Lyman (*puzzled—is she mad?*)   What river?

Theo   Where we went skinny-dipping with those geologists and their girls?

Lyman (*at a loss for a moment*)   Oh, you mean graduation night!

Theo   . . . The whole crowd swimming naked at the falls . . . and the girls all laughing in the darkness . . . ?

Lyman (*starting to smile but still uncomprehending*)   Oh sure . . . that was a great night!

Theo   I straddled you, and over your shoulder . . . did I dream this? I recall a white wall of limestone, rising straight out of the river . . . ?

Lyman   That's right, Devonian. It was full of fossils.

Theo   Yes! Beetle imprints, worm tracks, crustacea fifty million years old going straight up like a white temple wall . . . and we floated around below, like two frogs attached in the darkness . . . our wet eyelashes touching.

Lyman   Yes. It was beautiful. I'm glad you remember it that way.

Theo   Of course I do; I was never a Puritan, Lyman, it is simply a question of taste—that night was inspiring.

Lyman   Well, I never had taste, we both know that. But I won't lie to you, Theo—taste to me is what's left of life after people can't screw anymore.

Theo   You should have told me that thirty years ago.

Lyman   I didn't know it thirty years ago.

Theo   And do you remember what you said as we floated there?

Lyman (*hesitates*)   Yes.

Theo   You couldn't.

Lyman   I said, 'What could ever come between us?' Correct?

Theo (*surprised, derailed*)   . . . But did you mean that then? Please tell me the truth, it's important to me.

Lyman (*affected*)   Yes, I meant it.

Theo   Then . . . when did you begin to fool me?

Lyman   Please don't go on anymore . . .

Theo   I am trying to pinpoint when my life died. That's not unreasonable, is it?

Lyman   From my heart, Theo, I ask your pardon.

Theo   —When did Billie Holiday die?

Lyman (*perplexed*)   Billie Holiday?—oh I don't know, ten, twelve years ago? Why?

Theo *goes silent, staring into space. He is suddenly weeping at the sight of her suffering.*

Why do you want to know about Billie?

Bessie   All right, Mother, let's go, huh?

Lyman   I think it might be better if she talked it out . . .

Bessie   No one is interested in what you think. (*To* **Theo***:*) I want you to come now!

Lyman   Have mercy!

Bessie   You talking mercy?!

Lyman   For her, not me! Don't you hear what she's trying to say?—she loved me!

Bessie   How can you listen to this shit!

Lyman   How dare you! I gave you a damned fine life, Bessie!

Bessie   You have nothing to say anymore, you are nonsense!

Theo   Please, dear!—wait outside for a few minutes. (**Bessie***, seeing her adamance, strides out.*) You've torn out her heart. (**Lyman** *turns away trying not to weep.*) Was there some pleasure in making a fool of me? Why couldn't you have told me about this woman?

Lyman   I did try, many times, but . . . I guess it sounds crazy, but . . . I just couldn't bear to lose you.

Theo   But—(*with sudden, near-hysterical intensity*)—you were lying to me every day all these nine or ten years—what could you possibly lose?

Lyman (*determined not to flinch*)   . . . Your happiness.

Theo   *My* happiness! In God's name what are you talking about!

Lyman   Only the truth can help us, Theo—I think you were happier in those last years than ever in our marriage—you feel that, don't you?

She doesn't contradict.

May I tell you why? Because I was never bored being with you.

Theo   You'd been bored with me?

Lyman   Same as you'd been bored with me, dear . . . I'm talking about—you know—just normal marital boredom.

She seems obtuse to this, so he tries to explain.

You know, like at dinner—when I'd repeat some inane story you'd heard a thousand times . . . ? Like my grandfather losing three fingers under the Ninth Avenue trolley . . . ?

Theo   But I loved that story! I was *never* bored with you . . . stupid as that was.

Lyman (*now she just seems perverse*)   Theo, you were bored— it's no sin! Same as I was when, for instance, you'd start telling people for the ten thousandth time that . . . (*his charming laugh*) . . . as a minister's daughter you were not permitted to climb a tree and show off your panties?

Theo (*sternly resisting his charm*)   But I think that story describes a kind of society that has completely disappeared! That story has historical importance!

Lyman (*the full agony*)   That story is engraved in my flesh! . . . And I beg you, don't make this a moral dilemma. It is just common domestic tedium, dear, it is life, and there's no other woman I know who has the honesty and strength to accept it as life—if you wanted to!

Theo (*a pause; above her confusion, she is striving desperately to understand*)   And why do you say I was happier in these last years?

Lyman   Because you could see my contentment, and I was content . . .

Theo   Because she . . . ?

Lyman   Because whenever you started with your panties again I could still find you lovable, knowing that story was not going to be my entire and total fate till the day I died.

Theo   . . . Because she was waiting for you.

Lyman   Right.

Theo   You were never bored with *her?*

Lyman   Oh God yes! Sometimes even more than with you.

Theo (*with quick, intense, hopeful curiosity*)   Really! And what then?

Lyman   Then I would thank my luck that I had you to come back to.—I know how hard this is to understand, Theo.

Theo   No-no . . . I guess I've always known it.

Lyman   What.

Theo   You are some kind of . . . of giant clam.

Lyman   Clam?

Theo   Waiting on the bottom for whatever happens to fall from the ocean into your mouth; you are simply a craving, and that craving you call love. You are a kind of monster, and I think you even know it, don't you. I can almost pity you, Lyman. (*She turns to leave.*) I hope you make a good recovery. It's all very clear now, I'm glad I stayed.

Lyman   It's amazing—the minute the mystery of life appears, you think everything's cleared up.

Theo   There's no mystery to me, you have never loved anyone!

Lyman   Then explain to yourself how this worthless, loveless, treacherous clam could have single-handedly made two such different women happier than they'd ever been in their lives!

Theo   Really! (*Laughs, ending in a near-scream.*) Really and truly *happy?!*

Lyman   . . . In fact, if I dared admit the whole idiotic truth, the only one who suffered these past nine years—was *me!*

*An enormous echoing roar fills the theater—the roar of a lion. Light rises on **Bessie** looking front through field glasses; she is wearing shorts and a pith helmet and khaki safari jacket.*

Theo   *You suffering?*—oh dear God save us!

She is trying to sustain her bitter laughter and moves toward **Bessie***, and as she enters **Bessie**'s area **Theo**'s laughter dies off and she takes a pith helmet out of a picnic basket and puts it on. **Lyman**, slipping out of bed at the same time, follows **Theo**. There is no dialogue break.*

Lyman . . . What would you call it, then—having to look into your innocent, loving faces, when I knew the hollowness your happiness was based on? That isn't suffering?

He takes his place beside the two women, looking in the same direction out front, shading his eyes. With no break in dialogue . . .

Bessie (*looking through field glasses*) Good heavens, is he going to mount her *again?*

Lyman They don't call him the king of the beasts for nothing, honey.

Bessie Poor thing, how patient she is.

Theo (*taking the glasses from her*) Oh come, dear, she's not *only* patient.

Bessie (*spreading a tablecloth and picnic things on the ground*) But it's only once every half a year, isn't it?

Lyman Once that we *know* about.

Theo (*helping to spread the picnic*) Oh no, they're marvelously loyal couples.

Lyman No, dear, lions have harems—you're thinking of storks.

Bessie (*offering an egg*) Daddy?

Lyman (*sitting—happily eating*) I love you in those helmets, you look like two noble ladies on safari.

Theo (*stretching out on the ground*) The air here! The silence. These hills.

Bessie Thanks for bringing me, Daddy. I wish Harold could have been here.—Why do you look sad?

Lyman Just thinking. (*To* **Theo***:*) About monogamy—why you suppose we think of it as a higher form of life? (*She turns up to him . . . defensively*) . . . I mean I was just wondering.

Theo Well, it implies an intensification of love.

Lyman How about that, Bess? You had a lot of boyfriends before Harold, didn't you?

Bessie   Well . . . yes, I guess it is more intense with one.

Lyman   But how does that make it a higher form?

Theo   Monogamy strengthens the family; random screwing undermines it.

Lyman   But as one neurotic to another, what's so good about strengthening the family?

Theo   Well, for one thing it enhances liberty.

Bessie   Liberty? Really?

Theo   The family disciplines its members; when the family is weak the state has to move in; so the stronger the family the fewer the police. And that is why monogamy is a higher form.

Lyman   Jesus, did you just make that up? (*To* **Bessie**:) Isn't she marvelous? I'm giving her an A-plus!

Theo (*happily hurt*)   Oh shut up.

Lyman   But what about those Muslims? They're very big on stable families but a lot of them have two or three wives.

Theo   But only one is really the *wife*.

Lyman   Not according to my father—they often had two main women in Albania, one to run the house and the other for the bed. But they were both serious wives.

Theo   Your father's sociology was on a par with his morals. A wife to your father was a walking dish towel.

Lyman (*laughs, to* **Bessie**)   Your mother is a classical woman, you know why?

Bessie (*laughing delightedly*)   Why?

Lyman   Because she is always clear and consistent and . . .

Theo   . . . Rather boring.

He guffaws warmly, clapping his hands over his head in appreciation.

Bessie   You are not boring! (*Rushing to embrace* **Theo**.) Tell her she is not boring!

Lyman (*embracing* **Theo** *with* **Bessie**)   Theo, please . . . I swear I didn't mean boring!

Theo (*tearfully hurt*)   Well I'd rather be boring and clear than cute and stupid!

Lyman   Who asked you to be cute!—now please don't go on about it.

Theo   I wish I knew how to amuse you! Your eyes have been glazed over since we stepped onto this wretched continent!

Lyman (*guiltily stretching an awkward embrace toward her*)   I *love* this trip, and being with both of you . . . ! Theo, please!— now you are making me guilty!

The lion's roar interrupts and they all look front in shock.

Bessie   Is he heading here . . . ? Daddy!—he's trotting!

Guide's voice (*off, on bullhorn*)   You will have to come back to the car, everyone! At once!

Lyman   Quick! (*He pushes both women off.*)

Bessie (*on exiting*)   Daddy, come . . . !

Theo (*sensing he is remaining behind*)   Lyman . . . ?

Lyman   Go! (*He pushes* **Theo** *off, but turns back himself.*)

Guide's voice   Come back to the car at once, Mr. Felt!

Lion's roar—but closer now. **Lyman** *facing front and the lion, prepared to run for it but holding his ground.*

Mr. Felt, get back to the car!

Another roar.

Lyman (*eyes on the lion, shouting toward it with fear's exhilaration*)   I *am* happy, yes! That I'm married to Theodora and have Bessie . . . yes, *and* **Leah**, *too!*

Another roar!

Bessie (*from a distance*)   Daddy, please come here!

Lyman   And that I've made a mountain of money . . . yes, and have no impending lawsuits!

Bessie (*from a distance*)   Daddy . . . !

Lyman (*flinging his words toward the approaching beast, but crouched and ready to flee*)   . . . And that I don't sacrifice one day to things I don't believe in—including monogamy, yes!—(*arms thrown out, terror-inspired*)—I love my life, I am not guilty! I dare you to eat me, son of a bitch!

Immense roar! Wide-eyed, crouched now, and on the very verge of fleeing, he is watching the approaching lion—whose roar, as we now hear, has changed to a rather more relaxed guttural growling, much diminished; and **Lyman** *cautiously straightens up, and now turns triumphantly toward the women offstage. And* **Bessie** *flies out and throws her arms around him in ecstatic relief, kissing him.*

Bessie (*looking front*)   Daddy, he turned back! What did you do that for!

Theo *enters.*

Theo   He turned back! (*To* **Lyman***:*) How did you do that! (*To* **Bessie***:*) Did you see how he stopped and turned around? (*To* **Lyman***:*) What happened?

Lyman   I think I've lost my guilt! I think he sensed it! (*Half-laughing.*) Maybe lions don't eat happy people!

Theo   What are you talking about?

Lyman (*staring in wonder*)   I tell you his roar hit my teeth like voltage and suddenly it was so clear that . . . (*Turns to her.*) I've always been happy with you, Theo!—I just somehow couldn't accept it! But I am never going to apologize for my happiness again!—it's a miracle!

Theo (*with tears of gratitude, clasping her hands together prayerfully*)   Oh, Lyman! (*Rushing to kiss him.*) Oh, darling!

Lyman (*still riding his wave, holding out his hand to her*)   What old good friends we are, Theo! Put her there! (*She laughs and manfully shakes hands.*) What a *person* you are, what a grave and beautiful face you have!

Bessie   Oh, Daddy, that's so lovely!—you're just marvelous! (*She weeps.*)

Lyman   I worship this woman, Bessie! (*To* **Theo***:*) How the hell are we still together? (*To* **Bessie***:*)—Do you realize how she must love me to stand for my character?

Theo   Oh, this is what I always saw happening someday!—(*a sophisticated laugh*)—not with a lion, of course, but exactly this sudden flash of light . . . !

Lyman   The whole future is clear to me now! We are going to march happily into our late middle age, proudly, heads up! I'm going to build a totally selfish little cottage in the Caribbean and we'll fill it up with all the thick English novels we never got to finish . . . plus Proust!—and I'll buy two mopeds with little baskets on the handlebars for the shopping trips . . .

Theo   I knew it, I knew it!

Lyman   . . . And I'll spend every day with you—except maybe a week or so a month in the Elmira office!

Bessie   How fantastic, Mother!

Theo   Thank you, lion! Thank you, Africa! (*Turning to him.*) Lyman?

Lyman (*already mentally departing the scene*)   . . . Huh? Yes!

Theo   I am all new!

She throws her arms around him, burying her face in his neck. He looks front with an expression of deepening agony.

Bessie   This has been the most fantastic two weeks of my life! I love you, Daddy!

She rushes to him and with one arm he embraces her, the other around **Theo***. Tears are starting in his eyes.*

Are you weeping?

Lyman   Just amazement, honey . . . at my luck, I guess. Come, we'd better go back.

Somberly he turns them upstage; lights are changing, growing dimmer, and they walk into the darkness while he remains behind. Dim light reveals the **Nurse** *sitting near the bed.*

Nurse   The only thing I don't understand is why you married that woman, a smart man like you.

Lyman *stares ahead as* **Leah** *appears, isolated in light; she is in her fur coat, exactly as in Act One when she was about to go for an abortion. The* **Nurse** *remains in periphery, immobile.*

Leah   Yes, I suppose it could wait a week or so, but . . . really, Lyman, you know you're never going to leave her.

Lyman   You cancel the operation, okay? And I'm telling her tomorrow.

Leah   You're telling her what?

Lyman (*almost holding his breath*)   I will not rationalize you away. I have one life! I'm going to ask her for a divorce.

Leah   My God, Lyman!—But listen, I know your attachment to her . . .

Lyman (*kisses her hand*)   Please keep this baby. Will you? And stay home and cross your legs, you hear?

Leah   This is serious?

Lyman   This is serious. I'm asking her for a divorce.

Leah   Suddenly . . . why am I not sure I want to be a mother!— Do I, do you think?

Lyman   Yes you do, we think!

Kisses her. They laugh together. He turns to leave; she grasps his hands and presses them together between hers in a prayerful gesture; and facing heaven . . .

Leah   Please! Some good luck! (*To* **Lyman** *directly:*) Why is everything so dangerous! (*She gives him a violent kiss. She exits as* **Theo** *appears walking toward him; she is hiding something behind her back and smiling lovingly.* **Lyman** *looks solemn, prepared for the showdown.*)

Lyman   Theo, dear . . . There's something I have to tell you . . .

Theo (*holding out a cashmere sweater*)   Happy birthday!

Lyman (*startled*)   Hah? But it's not July, is it!

Theo   But it was so sinfully expensive I needed an excuse. (*Putting him into the sweater.*) Here . . . straighten it. It's not too big, is it? (*Stepping back to admire.*) It's gorgeous, look in the mirror!

Lyman   It's beautiful, thank you, dear. But listen, I really have something to . . .

Theo   My God, Lyman, you are simply magnificent! (*Linking arms with him and walking in her cumbersome way.*) I have another surprise—I got tickets for the Balanchine! And a table at Luigi's afterwards!

Lyman (*grimly screwing up his courage—and beginning to resent her domination*)   I have something to tell you, Theo, why do you make it so hard for me!

Theo   What. (*He is paralyzed.*) What is it? Has something happened? (*Alarmed now.*) Lyman!—(*asking*)—you went for your checkup!

Lyman (*about to explode*)   God's sake, no, it's not that!

Theo   Why is your face so gray? Please, what is it, you look terrified!

He moves away from her and her awful caring, and halts facing front. She remains behind and calls to him from the distance.

—My cousin Wilbur's still at Mass. General, we can go up there together . . . ! Please, darling, don't worry about anything . . . ! What is it, can't you tell me?

In total blockage—both in the past and in the present—he inhales deeply and lets out a gigantic long howl, arms raised, imploring heaven for relief. In effect, it blasts her out of his mind—she goes dark, and he is alone again.

Lyman (*to himself, facing front*)   No guts. That's the whole story. Courage! If I'd been honest for three consecutive minutes . . . No! I know what's wrong with me—I could never stand still for death! Which you've got to do by a certain age, or be ridiculous—you've got to stand there nobly and serene and let death run his tape out your arms and around your belly and up your crotch until he's got you fitted for that last black suit. And I can't, I won't! . . . So I'm left wrestling with this anachronistic energy which . . . (*as he leaps onto the bed, covering his left arm, crying out to the world*) . . . God has charged me with and I will use it till the dirt is shoveled into my mouth! Life! Life! Fuck death and dying!

Light widens, finding **Leah** *in the present, dressed differently than previously—in her fur coat—standing near the bed with the* **Nurse**, *listening to his shouts.*

Nurse   Don't be afraid, just wait a minute, he comes out of it. I'm sure he wants to see you.

Leah (*moving tentatively to the cast*)   Lyman? (*He looks at her with cloudy recognition.*) It's me, Leah.

Nurse *exits.* **Lyman** *now fully aware of* **Leah**.

Lyman   Leah! (*Turning away from her.*) Jesus, what have I done to you!—wait . . . (*A moment. He looks around.*) Was Theo here?

Leah   I think she's gone, I just got here.

Lyman   Oh, Leah, it's sitting on my chest like a bag of cement.

Leah   What is?

Lyman   My character.

Leah   Yes, well . . . it's pretty bad. Listen . . .

Lyman (*moved*)   Thanks for coming. You're a friend.

Leah   I only came about Benny. (*Frustrated, turns away.*) He's excited that he has a sister.

Lyman (*painful admiration*)   Oh that dear boy!

Leah   He's very badly mixed up, Lyman; he's seen us all on TV and the other kids tell him he has two mothers. He sits there and weeps. He keeps asking me are you coming home again. It's twisting my heart. I'm terrified if this isn't settled right it could screw up the rest of his life. (*Tears start.*) You're his idol, his god, Lyman!

Lyman   Oh, the wreckage, the wreckage . . .

Leah   Tell me the truth; whichever it is is okay but I just want to know—do you feel a responsibility or not?

Lyman (*flaring up, scared as much as indignant*)   How can you ask such a thing?

Leah   Why! That's a reasonable question!

Lyman   Now listen to me—I know I'm wrong and I'm wrong and I'm wrong but I did not throw you both across my saddle to rape you in my tent! You knew I was married, and you tried to make me love you, so I'm not entirely . . .

Leah   Lyman, if you're blaming me I'm going to sink through this floor!

Lyman   I'm talking about truth, not blame—this is not entirely a one-man disaster!

Leah   It's amazing, the minute you talk about truth you always come out looking better than anyone else!

Lyman   Now that's unfair!

Leah (*slight pause*)   I want to talk about Benny.

Lyman   You could bring him tomorrow if you like. But go ahead, we can talk now.

Leah (*a pause as she settles down*)   I'm thinking.

Lyman   Well stop thinking and bring him!

Leah (*with a flushed grin*)   Incidentally . . . they tell me you spent over an hour with your wife. Are you settling in there again?

Lyman   All she did was sit there telling me I'm a monster who never loved anybody.

Leah (*with a hard grin*)   And you reassured her otherwise, of course.

Lyman   Well, I did love her. And you know that better than anybody.

Leah   What a piece of work you are, Lyman, really—you go falling off a mountain and you still don't understand your hatred for that woman. It's monumental. It's . . . it's *oceanic.*

Lyman   What the hell is this now!

Leah   My dear man, in case it slipped your mind, when I was two months pregnant we went to New York and you picked the Carlyle Hotel to stay at—four blocks from your house! 'Loved her' . . . good G—!

A window begins to appear upstage with **Theo** *seated in profile, reading a book. He is staring as he emerges from the bed, turning to look up at the window . . .* **Leah** *goes on with no pause.*

What was all that about if it wasn't hatred!—And walking me past your front window with her sitting there . . . ? You had murder in you and you still do!—probably for me too!

Lyman (*glancing up at* **Theo** *in the window*)   But it didn't feel like murder at all. I was dancing the high wire on the edge of the world . . . finally risking everything to find myself! Strolling with you past my house, the autumn breeze, the lingerie in the Madison Avenue shop windows, the swish of . . . wasn't it a taffeta skirt you wore? . . . and my new baby coiled in your belly? —I'd beaten guilt forever! (*She is moving toward him, part of his recall.*) . . . And how languorous you were, your pregnant glory under the streetlamp!

She takes on the ease of that long-ago stroll, and . . .

Leah   Is that her?

Lyman *looks up at* **Theo***, then at* **Leah***, inspired, alive.*

Lyman   Oh Leah darling, how sexy you look against tall buildings.

Leah (*with a warm smile, taking his arm*)   You're tense, aren't you.

Lyman   Well, I lived here with her for so many years . . . You know?—I'd love to go in and say hello . . . But I don't have the guts . . .

Leah   Was she very upset when you told her?

Lyman (*tragically, but hesitates*)   Very, yes.

Leah   Well, maybe she'll think of marrying again.

Lyman   Marrying again? (*With a glance to the window; loosening her grip on his arm.*) I doubt it, somehow.

Leah (*with an intrigued smile*)   Mustn't we touch?

Lyman (*quickly regaining her arm*)   Of course! (*They start walking away.*)

Leah   I'd love to meet her sometime . . . just as friends.

Lyman   You might. (*Halts. A strange determination suddenly.*) Listen, I'd like to see if I can go in and say hello.

Leah   Why not! You don't want me to come, do you?

Lyman   Not just yet. Would you mind a lot?

Leah   Why! I'm glad that you still have feeling for her.

Lyman   God, you have balls! I'll see you back at the hotel in twenty minutes, okay?

Leah   Take your time! I'll play with all that gorgeous underwear you bought. (*Touching her belly.*) I'm so contented, Lyman!

She turns and walks toward the cast, which lights up. He remains below the window, staring at her departing figure.

Lyman (*alone*)   Why is it, the happier she is the sadder I get? It's this damned *objectivity!*—Why can't I just dive in and swim in my happiness! (*Now he looks up at* **Theo**, *and his heart sinks. Leaps up with violent determination.*) Idiot!—love her! Now that she can't deprive you anymore let love flow to your wise and wonderful wife! (*He rushes toward* **Theo**, *but then turns away in terror, walking around in a circle and blowing out air and covering his face.*) Guilt, burn in hell! (*Now he again hurries toward the window . . . which disappears, as she rises, setting her book down, startled.*)

Theo   Lyman! —You said Tuesday, didn't you?

He takes her in his arms, kisses her frantically. She is surprised and happy.

Lyman   What a handsome lady! Theo, you are God's handwriting.

Theo   Ralph Waldo Emerson.

Lyman   Someday I'm going to swipe an image you never heard of! (*Laughing, in a comradely style, embraces her closely as he takes her to a seat—stoking up a certain excited intimacy here.*) Listen, I just hitched a ride down with this pilot in his new Cessna—I have meetings up there starting seven-thirty tomorrow but I just had to astonish you.

Theo   You flew in a small plane *at night?*

Lyman   That whole fear was guilt, Theo—I thought I *deserved* to crash. But I deserve to live because I am not a bad guy and I love you.

Theo   Well, I'm floating away! When must you go back?

Lyman   Now.

Theo (*near laughter at the absurdity*)   Can't we even chat?

Lyman   Let me call that I'm on my way. (*Dials a phone.*)

Theo   I'll drive you to the airport.

Lyman   No, he's picking me up at the Carlyle . . . Hello?

Lights up on **Leah**, *holding a phone.*

Leah   Darling!

Lyman   Be there in ten minutes.

Leah (*puzzled*)   Oh? Okay. Why are you calling?

Lyman   Just to make sure you didn't forget me and took off.

Leah   Your jealousy is so comforting!—You know, she made a very dignified picture, reading in the window—it was like an Edward Hopper, kind of haunted.

Lyman   Yes. Well, I'm leaving right now. (*Hangs up.*)

Theo   You won't forget about dinner Thursday with Leona and Gilbert . . . he's gotten his hearing aid so it won't be so bad.

Lyman (*with a certain solemnity, taking her hands*)   I just had to steal this extra look at you . . . life's so stupidly short, Theo.

Theo (*happily*)   Why must death always sit on your shoulder when you've got more life in you than anybody! (*Ruffling his hair.*) In fact, you're kind of sparkly tonight.

Lyman (*responding to her acceptance*)   Listen, we have time to make love.

Theo (*with a surprised, delighted laugh*)   I wish I knew what's come over you!

Lyman   The realization of what a sweet piece of ass my wife is. (*He starts to lead her.*)

Theo   I bet it's the new office in Elmira—new beginnings are always so exciting! There's such power in you, Lyman.

Lyman (*turning her to him, he kisses her mouth*)   Yes, we're going to do great business up there! Tell me something—has there ever been a god who was guilty?

Theo   Gods are never guilty, that's why they're gods.

Lyman   It feels like the moon's in my belly and the sun's in my mouth and I'm shining down on the world. (*Laughs with a self-mocking charm.*) . . . A regular planetary flashlight! Come! (*And laughing in high tension takes her hand and moves her into darkness . . .*)

Theo   Oh, Lyman—how wonderfully, endlessly changing you are!

Blackout.

Scene Three

Lights up on **Leah** *in hospital room;* **Lyman** *is returning to the bed.*

Leah   So you bopped her that night.

Lyman   What can I say?

Leah   And when you came back to the hotel, didn't we . . . ?

Lyman   I couldn't help myself, you both looked absolutely gorgeous! How can that be evil?

Leah (*with a sigh*)   There's just no end to you, is there. —Listen, I came to talk business; I want the house transferred to my name . . .

Lyman   *What?*

Leah   . . . Immediately. I know how much feeling you put into it but I want the security for Benny's sake.

Lyman   Leah, I beg you to wait with that . . .

Leah   I will not wait with that! And I want my business returned to me.

Lyman   That'll be complicated—it's many times bigger than when I took it over . . .

Leah   I want it back! I would have expanded without you! I'm not going to be a *total* fool! I will sue you!

Lyman (*with a very uncertain grin*)   You'd really sue me?

Leah (*searching in her pocketbook*)   I'm not fooling around, Lyman. You've hurt me very deeply . . . (*She breaks off, holding back tears. She takes out a sheet of paper.*)

Lyman (*forced to turn from her*)   Jesus, how I hate to see you cry.

Leah   I have something I want you to sign.

Lyman   To *sign?*

Leah   It's a quit-claim on the house and my business. Will you read it?

Lyman   You're not serious.

Leah   I had Ted Lester draw it up. Here, read it.

Lyman   I know what a quit-claim is, don't tell me to read a quit-claim. How can you do this?

Leah   We aren't married and I don't want you making claims on me.

Lyman   And . . . and what about Benny. You don't mean you're taking Benny from me . . .

Leah   I . . .

Lyman   I want you to bring him here tomorrow morning so I can talk to him.

Leah   Just a minute . . .

Lyman   No! You're going to bring him, Leah . . .

Leah   Now you listen to me! I will not allow you to see him until I know what you intend to say to him about all this. I've also been through it with my father's old lawyer and you haven't a legal leg to stand on.

Lyman   I'll tell him the truth—I love him.

Leah   You mean it's all right to lie and deceive people you love? He's all I have now, Lyman, I am not going to see him go crazy!

Lyman   Now you stop that! I did a helluva lot more than lie to him . . .

Leah (*outpouring*)   You lied to him!—why don't you seem to register this? . . . To buy him the pony, and teach him to ski, and take him up in the glider . . . you made him worship you—when you knew what you knew! That was cruelty!

Lyman   All right, what do you think I should tell him?

Leah   That you beg his pardon and say he mustn't follow your example because lying to people injures them.

Lyman   I am not turning myself into a pile of shit in front of my son's face! If I can teach him anything now it's to have the guts to be true to himself! That's all that matters!

Leah   Even if he has to betray the whole world to do it?

Lyman   Only the truth is sacred, Leah!—to hold back nothing!

Leah   You must be crazy—you hold back everything! You really don't know right from wrong, do you!

Lyman   Jesus Christ, you sound like Theo!

Leah   Well maybe it's what happens to people who marry you! Look—I don't think it's a good idea at the moment . . .

Lyman   I have a right to see my son!

Leah   I won't have him copying you, Lyman, it will destroy his life! I'm leaving! (*She starts to leave.*)

Lyman   You bring me Benny or I'll . . . I'll sue you, god dammit!

Enter **Bessie** *alone. She is extremely tense and anxious.*

Bessie   Oh, good, I was hoping you'd still be here. Listen . . .

Leah   I was just going . . .

Bessie   Oh please wait! My mother's had an attack of some kind . . .

Lyman   My God, what is it!

Bessie   They're looking at her in a room down the hall. She's a little delusionary and talks about taking him home with her, and I think it would help for her to see you're still together.

Leah   But we're not at all together . . .

Lyman   Wait! Why must it be delusion—maybe she really wants me back!

Bessie (*with a frustrated stamp of her foot*)   I want her out of here and home!

Lyman   I am not a monster, Bessie! My God, where did all this cruelty come from!

Leah   He wants her, you see . . .

Lyman   I want you both!

Bessie (*a hysterical overtone, screaming*)   Will you once in your life think of another human being!

Tom *and* **Theo** *enter with the* **Nurse***; he has* **Theo** *by the arm. She has a heightened, seeing air about her, but a fixed, dead smile, and her head trembles.*

Lyman   Theo!—come, sit her down, Tom!

Leah (*to* **Bessie***, fearfully*)   I really feel I ought to go . . .

Theo   Oh, I wish you could stay for a few minutes! (*To* **Nurse***:*) Please get a chair for Mrs. Felt.

The reference causes surprise in **Bessie***.* **Leah** *looks quickly to* **Bessie***, perplexed because this is the opposite of what* **Bessie** *and* **Theo** *wished.* **Lyman** *is immensely encouraged. The* **Nurse***, as she goes out for the chair, glances about, perplexed.*

Pleasantly   Well! Here we are all together.

Slight pause.

Tom   She's had a little . . . incident, Lyman. (*To* **Bessie***:*) I've arranged for a plane; the three of us can fly down together.

Bessie   Oh good. —We're ready to leave whenever you say, Mother.

Lyman   Thanks, Theo . . . for coming.

Theo (*turns to him, smiling blankly*)   Socialism is dead.

Lyman   Beg your pardon?

Theo   And Christianity is finished, so . . . (*Searches*) . . . there really is nothing left to . . . to . . . to defend. Except simplicity? (*She* *crosses her legs, and her coat falls partially open, revealing a bare thigh.*)

Bessie   Mother!—where's your skirt?

Theo   I'm comfortable, it's all right . . .

Nurse *enters with a chair.*

Bessie   She must have left her skirt in that room she was just in—would you get it, please?

Nurse, *perplexed again, exits.*

Theo (*to* **Leah**)   I wish I hadn't carried on that way . . . I'm sorry. I've really nothing against you personally, I just never cared for your *type*. The surprise is what threw me, I mean that you were actually married. But I think you are rather an interesting person . . . I was just unprepared, but I'm seeing things much clearer now. Yes. (*Breaks off.*) Do you see the *Village Voice* up here?

Leah   Yes, occasionally.

Theo   There was a strange interview some years back with Isaac Bashevis Singer, the novelist? The interviewer was a woman whose husband had left her for another woman, and she couldn't understand why. And Singer said, "Maybe he liked her hole better." I was shocked at the time, really outraged—you know, that he'd gotten a Nobel; but now I think it was courageous to have said that, because it's probably true. Courage . . . courage and directness are always the main thing!

Nurse *enters, offers* **Theo** *the skirt.*

Nurse   Can I help you on with it?

Theo (*takes the skirt, looks at it without recognition, and drops it on the floor*)   I can't remember if I called you Leah or Mrs. Felt.

Leah   I'm not really Mrs. Felt.

Theo (*with a pleasant social smile*)   Well, you are *a* Mrs. Felt; perhaps that's all one can hope for when we are so interchangeable—

who knows anymore which Mrs. Felt will be coming down for breakfast! (*Short pause.*) Your boy needs his father, I imagine.

Leah   Well . . . yes, but . . .

Theo   Then he should be here with you, shouldn't he. We must all be realistic now. (*To* **Lyman***:*) You can come up here whenever you want to . . . if that's what you'd really like.

Bessie (*to* **Tom**)   She's really too ill for this. —Come, Mother, we're going.

Theo   I'm not at all ill. (*To* **Lyman***:*) I can say 'fuck,' you know. I never cared for the word but I'm sure she has her limitations too. I can say 'Fuck me, Lyman,' 'Fuck you, Lyman'; whatever.

Lyman *is silent in guilty anguish.*

Bessie (*to* **Lyman***, furiously*)   Will you tell her to leave? Just out of respect, out of friendship!

Lyman   Yes. (*Delicately.*) She's right, Theo, I think that would be the best . . .

Theo (*to* **Bessie**)   But I can take better care of him at home. (*To* **Leah***:*) I really have nothing to do, and you're busy, I imagine . . .

Bessie   Tom, will you . . .

Tom   Why don't we let her say what's on her mind?

Theo (*to* **Bessie**)   I want to start being real—he had every right to resent me. Truly. What did I ever do but correct him? (*To* **Leah***:*) You don't correct him, do you. You like him as he is, even now, don't you. And that's the secret, isn't it. (*To* **Lyman***:*) Well I can do that. I don't need to correct you . . . or pretend to . . .

Bessie   I can't bear this, Mother!

Theo   But this is our *life,* Bessie dear; you must bear it. —I think I've always pretty well known what he was doing. Somewhere inside we all really know everything, don't we? But one has to live, darling—one has to live . . . in the same house, the same bed. And so one learns to tolerate . . . it's a good thing to tolerate . . . (*A furious shout.*) And tolerate, and tolerate!

Bessie (*terrified for her mother*)   Daddy, please . . . tell her to go!

Lyman   But she's telling the truth!

Leah (*suddenly filling up*)   You poor woman! (*To him:*) What a bastard you are; one honest sentence from you and none of this would have happened, it's despicable! (*Appealing to* **Theo***:*) I'm so sorry about it, Mrs. Felt . . .

Theo   No-no . . . he's absolutely right—he's always said it—it's life I can't trust! But you—you trust it, and that's why you *should* win out.

Leah   But it's not true—I never really trusted him! Not really! I always knew there was something dreadful wriggling around underneath! (*In full revolt now.*) I'll tell you the goddamned truth, I never really wanted to marry anybody! I've never known one happy couple! —Listen, you mustn't blame yourself, the whole damned thing doesn't work, it never works. . . which I knew and went ahead and did it anyway and I'll never understand why!

Lyman   Because if you hadn't married me you wouldn't have kept Benny, that's why. (*She can't find words.*) You wouldn't have had Benny or this last nine years of your happiness. Shit that I am, I helped you become the woman you always wanted to be, instead of . . . (*Catches himself.*) Well, what's the difference?

Leah   No, don't stop—instead of what? What did you save me from?

Lyman (*accepting her challenge*)   All right . . . from all those lonely postcoital showerbaths, and the pointless pillow talk and the boxes of heartless condoms beside your bed . . . !

Leah (*speechless*)   Well now!

Lyman   I'm sick of this crap, Leah! —You got a little something out of this despicable treachery!

Theo   That's a terrible thing to say to the woman.

Lyman   But the truth is terrible, what else have you just been saying? It's terrible because it's embarrassing, but the truth is always embarrassing or it isn't the truth! —You tolerated me because you loved me, dear, but wasn't it also the good life that I gave you? —Well, what's wrong with that? Aren't women people? Don't people love comfort and power? I don't understand the disgrace here!

Bessie (*to both women*)   Why are you still sitting here, don't you have any pride! (*To* **Leah***:*) This is disgusting!

Leah   Will you please stop this high moral tone? I have business with him, so I have to talk to him! —I'll go out of my mind here! Am I being accused of something?

Off to the side, **Tom** *bends his head over clasped hands, eyes shut.*

Bessie   You shouldn't be in the same room with him!

Leah (*rattled*)   I just explained that, didn't I? *What the hell do you want?*

Lyman (*crying out, voice cracking with a sob*)   She wants her father back!

Bessie   You son of a bitch! (*Raises her fists, then weeps helplessly.*)

Lyman   I love you—Bessie!—all of you!

Bessie   You ought to be killed!

Lyman   You are all magnificent!

Bessie *bursts into tears. A helpless river of grief, which now overflows to sweep up* **Lyman***; then* **Leah** *is carried away by the wave of weeping. All strategies collapse as finally* **Theo** *is infected. The four of them are helplessly covering their faces. It is a veritable mass keening, a funerary explosion of grief each for his or her own condition, for love's frustration and for the end of all their capacity to reason.* **Tom** *has turned from them, head bent in prayer, hands clasped, eyes shut.*

Lyman (*his eye falls on* **Theo***'s bare leg*)   Tom, please!—get her to put some clothes on . . . (*Breaks off.*) Are you praying, for Christ's sake?

Tom (*staring ahead*)   There is no way to go forward. You must all stop loving him. You must or he will destroy you. He is an endless string attached to nothing.

Lyman   Who is not an endless string? Who is sworn to some high golden purpose now—lawyers? Why are you all talking nonsense?

Tom   —Theo needs help now, Lyman, and I don't want a conflict, so I don't see how I can go on representing you.

Lyman   Of course not, I am not worthy. (*A shout, but with the strain of his loss, his inability to connect.*)—But I *am* human, and proud of it!—yes, of the glory and the shit! The truth, the truth is holy!

Tom (*exploding*)   Is it. Well! Then you'll admit that you moved that barrier aside yourself, and drove onto that sheet of ice? That's the truth, isn't it?

Lyman (*instant's hesitation*)   That was not suicide—I am not a cop-out!

Tom   Why is it a cop-out? Your shame finally caught up with you—or is that too true for comfort? Your shame is the best part of you, for God's sake, why do you pretend you're beyond it? (*Breaks off, giving it up.*) I'm ready to go, Theo.

Lyman (*suddenly struck*)   One more moment—I beg you all. Before you leave me . . . please. I'd like to tell you something.

Bessie (*quietly relentless*)   Mother?

She raises **Theo** *to her feet. Her head is trembling. She turns to* **Lyman**.

Lyman   I'm asking you to hear me out, Theo. I see what happened.

Theo   I have nothing left in me anymore, Lyman.

Bessie *takes her by the arm to go.* **Leah** *stands, as though to leave.*

Lyman   I beg you, Leah, two minutes. I have to tell you this!

Leah (*an evasive color*)   I have work in the office . . .

Lyman (*losing control*)   Two minutes, Leah? Before you take away my son because of my unworthiness? (*Pause. Something simple, authentic in his tone stops them all.*) Here is how I got on the Mount Morgan road. I kept calling you, Leah, from the Howard Johnson's to tell you I'd be staying over because of the storm . . . but the line was busy. So I went to bed, but it was busy . . . over an hour . . . more! And I started to ask the operator to cut in as an emergency when . . . (*Breaks off.*) I remembered what you once said to me . . .

Leah   I was talking to . . .

Lyman (*in quick fury*)   It doesn't matter, I'm not accusing you, or defending myself either, I'm telling you what *happened!*—please let me finish!

Leah   I was talking to my brother!

Lyman   In Japan, for over an hour?

Leah   He just got back on Monday.

Lyman   Well it doesn't matter!

Leah   It certainly does matter!

Lyman   Please let me finish, Leah; remember you once said . . . 'I might lie to you,' remember that? Way at the beginning? It seemed so wonderful then . . . that you could be so honest; but now, on my back in that room, I started to die.

Leah   I don't want to hear anymore!

Theo, **Bessie** *are moving out.*

Lyman   Wait! Please! I haven't made my point! (*Something new, genuine in his voice stops them.*) I want to stop lying. It's simple. (*A visionary look.*) On my back in that bed, the snow piling up outside . . . the wind howling at my window—this whole nine-year commute suddenly seemed so ludicrous, it was suddenly laughable. I couldn't understand why I'd done it. And somehow I realized that I had no feeling left . . . for myself or anyone . . . I was a corpse on that bed. And I got dressed and drove back into the storm. I don't know—maybe I did want to die, except that what I really thought, Leah . . . was that if I walked in two, three in the morning out of a roaring blizzard like that . . . you'd believe how I needed you. And then I would believe it too, and I'd come back to life again. Unless . . . (*Turns to* **Tom**.) I just wanted the end of it all. (*To the women:*) But I swear to you . . . looking at you now, Theo, and Leah, and you, Bessie . . . I have never felt the love that I feel right now. But I've harmed you and I know it. —And one more thing; I can't leave you with a lie—the truth is that in some miserable, dark corner of my soul I still don't see why I am condemned. I bless you all. (*He weeps helplessly.*)

Bessie *turns* **Theo** *to leave.*

Theo   . . . Say goodbye to him, dear.

Bessie (*dry-eyed now; her feeling clearer, she has a close to impersonal sound*)   I hope you're better soon, Daddy. Goodbye.

*She takes her mother's arm—***Theo** *no longer resists as they move out into darkness. He turns to* **Leah.**

Lyman   Oh Leah, say something tough and honest . . . the way you can.

Leah   I don't know if I'll ever believe anything . . . or anybody, again.

Lyman   Oh no. No!—I haven't done that!

A great weeping sweeps **Leah** *and she rushes out.*

Leah! Leah! Don't say I've done that!

But she is gone.

Tom   Talk to you soon.

He sees that **Lyman** *is lost in space, and he goes out. The* **Nurse** *comes from her corner to* **Lyman**.

Nurse   You got pain?

He doesn't reply.

I'll get you something to smooth you out.

Lyman   Don't leave me alone, okay?—for a little while? Please, sit with me. (*Pats the mattress. She approaches the bed but remains standing.*)

I want to thank you, Logan. I won't forget your warmth, especially. A woman's warmth is the last magic, you're a piece of sun. —Tell me . . . when you're out there on the ice with your husband and your boy . . . what do you talk about?

Nurse   . . . Well, let's see . . . this last time we all bought us some shoes at that big Knapp Shoe Outlet up there?—they're seconds, but you can't tell them from new.

Lyman   So you talked about your new shoes?

Nurse   Well, they're great buys.

Lyman   Right. That . . . that's just wonderful to do that. I don't know why, but it just is.

Nurse   I'll be right back. (*She starts away.*)

Lyman   Hate me?

Nurse (*with an embarrassed shrug*)   I don't know. I got to think about it.

Lyman   Come right back, huh? I'm still a little . . . shaky.

She leans down and kisses his forehead.

Why'd you do that?

Nurse (*shrugs*)   No reason.

She exits.

Lyman (*painful wonder and longing in his face, his eyes wide, alive . . .*)   What a miracle everything is! Absolutely everything! . . . Imagine . . . three of them sitting out there together on that lake, talking about their shoes! (*He begins to weep, but quickly catches himself.*) Now learn loneliness. But cheerfully. Because you earned it, kid, all by yourself. Yes. You have found Lyman at last! So . . . cheer up!

Blackout.

Notes

Act One

5   *Eisenhower.* Dwight David Eisenhower (1890–1969) was a General in the Army during the Second World War and became the 34th President of the US from the Republican Party from 1953–1961. When Lyman asks about him to the nurse (who is black), it's an ironic reference since Eisenhower was known for not using his moral authority to help advance black civil rights, even once being dismissive of Martin Luther King Jr.

6   *Earl Hines.* Earl Kenneth Hines, byname *Fatha* (1903–1983), was an American jazz pianist, and bandleader who helped shape the history of the genre in the US.

6   *Jimmy Baldwin.* A reference to James Baldwin (1924–1987), an African-American essayist, novelist, playwright and poet whose essays are seminal on matters of race, poverty and sexuality. The *I'm Not Your Negro* documentary produced in 2016 and directed by Raoul Peck has recently brought him into the spotlight again.

12   *East Seventy-fourth Street.* Considered one the most expensive neighbourhoods in the Upper East Side of New York City.

12   *The Carlyle.* A luxury hotel on New York's Upper East Side. Once nicknamed 'New York White House' (President JFK owned an apartment on the 34th floor for the last ten years of his life), it has had famous guests like Prince Harry, Meghan Markle, Princess Diana, Michael Jackson, and many others.

12   *Elmira.* The largest city and the county seat of Chemung County, New York.

13   *Harold Lamb.* This is a fictional name for the painter in the play.

14   *Reno.* The city in which they marry is an ironic element as it is located in one of America's most liberal states, Nevada. The 'City of Sin', Las Vegas, is also located in the same state, and is known for embracing gambling, shopping in luxury stores, as well as being a great hub where magnates, billionaires and people from the financial sector like to have fun.

19   *My father died at fifty-three.* His father will be his nostalgic reference of success throughout the play.

20   *Quaker.* Quakers belong to a historically Protestant Christian set of denominations known formally as the Religious Society of Friends. Focusing on the inner experience, they reject sacraments, rituals and

formal ministry. Historically they have promoted many causes for social reform.

21   *Park Avenue.* One of the most famous avenues in New York City. Iconic structures such as the Waldorf-Astoria, the Pan Am building and Grand Central Station are found there.

22   *Darling, it comes down to being a single parent and I just don't want that.* This reflects the conservative ideology to which the play relates where an unmarried woman would be easily judged and scorned.

30   *She's the worst generation in our history.* Here Theodora criticized aspects that are still widely criticized by conservatives to this date.

Act Two

39   *Billie Holiday.* Eleanora Fagan (1915–1959), known professionally as Billie Holiday, was an American jazz and swing music singer, and is still considered one of the most influential voices of all times. One of her signature songs is 'Strange Fruit' (1939).

41   *Montauk.* Located on the Atlantic Ocean and Block Island Sound it is the most expensive beach destination in the US.

42   *Finnegans Wake.* Considered James Joyce's most difficult novel written in 1939.

46   *Gefilte fish.* A typical dish of Eastern European Jewish cuisine (Ashkenazi) made from a poached mixture of ground deboned fish, such as carp, pike or whitefish. It is popular on Shabbat and Jewish holidays.

50   *Audubon Society.* This is a real non-governmental organization (NGO) founded in 1905 that is still active and focuses on nature and animal protection. Its insertion in the play works as an ironic element since the Reagan administration was one of the biggest opponents of the measures against deforestation, climate change, etc.

64   *Mass. General.* Massachusetts General Hospital is a hospital in Boston with an outstanding reputation. Attached to Harvard University it has consistently been placed among the top five hospitals on the Honor Roll since its inception in 1990.

67   *Madison Avenue.* An avenue in the borough of Manhattan known as the shopping centre for wealthy people from all over the world.

69   *Ralph Waldo Emerson.* Emerson (1803–1882) was an American abolitionist, essayist, lecturer, philosopher and poet. The full quotation to which Lyman refers is: 'Never lose an opportunity of seeing anything that is beautiful, for beauty is God's handwriting'.

70 *Edward Hopper*. American realist painter (1882–1967) who depicted everyday urban scenes that showed the strangeness of familiar surroundings. He strongly influenced the Pop Art and New Realist painters of the 1960s and 1970s.

75 *Village Voice*. Founded in 1955, this is the nation's first alternative weekly newspaper, covering the counterculture, politics and the vast cultural landscape up to now.

75 *Isaac Bashevis Singer*. A Polish-born Jewish-American writer (1902–1991) who initially wrote in Yiddish and afterwards translated himself to English. One of his most famous short stories 'Yentl, the Yeshiva Boy' was adapted to the stage and to film, the latter featuring Barbra Streisand in the lead role and as its producer and director. Singer also won the Nobel Prize in 1978.